CFA Institute

AF885235

CFA INSTITUTE INDUSTRY GUIDES

THE AUTOMOTIVE INDUSTRY

by Adam Kindreich, CFA

ISBN 978-1-942713-14-2
August 2015

ABOUT THE AUTHOR

Adam Kindreich, CFA, has been an equity research analyst for more than two decades; he worked on the sell side for 13 years and the buy side for 10 years. He started work as a graduate trainee economist at a UK investment bank. In 1991, Mr. Kindreich moved into equity research in Paris with a local broker. After spending time analyzing French stocks, he began specializing in French consumer stocks. Mr. Kindreich has also worked as a global consumer buy-side analyst at a private bank in Geneva and at a global institutional investment manager in the Netherlands. He holds an MA degree in economics/mathematics from the University of St. Andrews. Mr. Kindreich also holds a UK Investment Management Certificate and has been an active volunteer with CFA Institute since 2011.

CFA INSTITUTE INDUSTRY GUIDES

THESE OTHER INDUSTRY GUIDES ARE AVAILABLE FROM CFA INSTITUTE

THE ASSET MANAGEMENT INDUSTRY
Owen Concannon, CFA
April 2015

THE REIT INDUSTRY
Irfan Younus, CFA
April 2015

THE MACHINERY INDUSTRY
Anthony M. Fiore, CFA
September 2013

THE TOBACCO INDUSTRY
Ade Roberts, CFA
April 2014

THE PHARMACEUTICAL INDUSTRY
Marietta Miemietz, CFA
November 2013

CONTENTS

AUTOMOTIVE MANUFACTURING

INDUSTRY OVERVIEW

The automotive industry is one that all investors can easily relate to because of its significance in everyday life and the relevance and even necessity of its product. This global industry encompasses car and component manufacturing, including tires (which are usually considered apart from other automotive components because of their special characteristics). This report begins by looking at car manufacturing and its characteristics.

Car manufacturers are often abbreviated as OEMs (original equipment manufacturers).[1] The general characteristics and recent trends in the automotive industry include the following:

- The industry is capital intensive and highly cyclical, so it tends to be difficult for investors to forecast.
- The car industry, being one of the first industries to display the latest cyclical trends, typically leads the economic cycle.
- The industry experiences a high degree of unpredictability from sudden regulation, demand changes, market shifts, and the unknown success of future model launches.
- Globalization of the industry, for both OEMs and component suppliers, is increasing.
- The growing importance of emerging markets, especially China, is notable.
- Price competition is intense, with most markets being fragmented in product terms and having no dominant players.
- More efficient manufacturing techniques, including platform manufacture and modularity, have begun.
- Government interventions and political interference (e.g., scrappage schemes to support demand, subsidies for new manufacturing plants) continue.
- A convergence is occurring in product quality and growing product standardization across OEMs.

[1]This report is limited to manufacturers. It does not consider car dealerships, which are part of the distribution or retail side of the business and operate with a different business model and different industry dynamics.

- Alliances and industrial partnerships, not mergers and acquisitions, are used to achieve scale.
- Companies are focusing on their core businesses—car and component manufacture—with the sale of noncore divisions.
- Rationalization of the supplier base has involved small, regionally based suppliers being replaced by global suppliers.

The preceding list is not exhaustive but provides a sampling of key aspects of the automotive industry.

Auto manufacturing annual industry revenue was approximately USD2,100 billion in 2014. This figure is based on global light vehicle sales of close to 88 million units at an average sales price (by manufacturers to dealers) of slightly under USD24,000. Approximately 10 million jobs are directly involved in car manufacturing worldwide, accounting for 5% of manufacturing employment, and another 50 million jobs are indirectly related to the car industry. Furthermore, the industry is a major consumer of such key commodities as copper, aluminum, and steel. Thus, car manufacturing and its suppliers occupy a significant place in the global economy.

CAR MANUFACTURERS: MODEL CLASSIFICATION

Cars can be classified in a number of ways, depending on the market segment to which they belong. Cars are usually classified according to size, length, wheelbase, and engine size. Letters for attributes range from A, denoting the smallest, most basic, and least expensive cars, up to F, denoting a large luxury car. Specialist vehicles are given separate letterings that depend on their use and particular characteristics.

Many organizations have their own lettering systems. **Exhibit 1** shows the European Commission's classification, with examples of particular models in each class.

Exhibit 2 shows a typical split of sales by market segment for several car manufacturers.

Manufacturers often keep their plans for car model launches confidential as to exact details and expected changes and indicate to investors only the segment in which new launches will be made.

AUTO MANUFACTURING: SALES, PRODUCTION, AND VEHICLES IN USE

In 2014, global car sales reached 88.2 million units, marking the fifth consecutive year of growth since the global financial crisis year of 2009 and, as indicated in **Exhibit 3**, representing approximately 3% growth over 2013.

Exhibit 1. Light Vehicle Segment Classification

Segment	Description	Model Examples
A	Mini cars	Tata Nano, Smart Fortwo, Fiat 500, Toyota Aygo
B	Small cars	Ford Fiesta, Opel Corsa, Peugeot 207, Volkswagen Polo
C	Medium cars	Chevrolet Cruze, Ford Focus, Honda Civic, Toyota Corolla
D	Large cars	Ford Fusion, Hyundai Sonata, Audi A4, BMW 3
E	Executive cars	Chevrolet Impala, Toyota Avalon, Ford Taurus, Volvo S80
F	Luxury cars	Audi A8, BMW 7, Mercedes-Benz S, Porsche Panamera, Tesla S
S	Sport coupés	BMW 6, Audi TT, Porsche Boxster, Mercedes-Benz CLK
M	Multipurpose cars	Volkswagen Touran, Renault Scenic, Opel Zafira, Ford C-Max
J	Sport utility cars/ off-road vehicles	Ford EcoSport, Chevrolet Equinox, Jeep Wrangler
—	Pick-up trucks	Ford Ranger, Dodge Ram, Chevrolet Montana, Fiat Strada

Source: European Commission.

Exhibit 2. Sales Exposure by Segment, 2013

	A + B + C	D + E + F	RV[a]	Others
Honda	45.9%	18.5%	34.1%	1.5%
Toyota	40.1	15.6	31.0	13.3
Renault	49.1	21.0	16.3	13.6
Volkswagen	61.6	19.4	12.8	6.2
Hyundai[b]	55.3	18.3	18.9	7.5

[a]Recreational vehicles. [b]Hyundai data are for 2014.
Source: Hyundai Motor Company Investor Presentation (May 2015): http://worldwide.hyundai.com/wcm/idc/groups/sggeneralcontent/@hmc/documents/sitecontent/mdaw/mdk4/~edisp/hw098669.pdf.

In terms of car sales, **Exhibit 4** shows the two largest markets in the world, China and the United States, after which individual markets drop sharply in terms

Exhibit 3. Global Light Vehicle Sales, 2005–2014

Year	Units (millions)
2005	65.9
2006	68.4
2007	71.6
2008	68.3
2009	65.6
2010	75.0
2011	78.2
2012	82.2
2013	85.6
2014	88.2

Note: The category "light vehicle" includes passenger cars and commercial vehicles.
Source: International Organization of Motor Vehicle Manufacturers, "2005–2014 Sales Statistics" (www.oica.net/category/sales-statistics).

Exhibit 4. Global Light Vehicle Sales by Country, 2014

Country	Units (millions)
China	23.5
United States	16.8
Japan	5.6
Brazil	3.5
Germany	3.4
India	3.2
United Kingdom	2.8
Russia	2.5
France	2.2
Canada	1.9
South Korea	1.7
Italy	1.5
Iran	1.3
Indonesia	1.2
Mexico	1.2
Australia	1.1

Source: International Organization of Motor Vehicle Manufacturers, "2005–2014 Sales Statistics" (www.oica.net/category/sales-statistics).

of size. For a long time, the United States was the world's largest car market by sales volume, but it was surpassed by China in 2009.

Cars are not necessarily produced in the markets in which they are sold, although there is usually a significant overlap between the volumes produced and sold in a market. At the same time, a great deal of exporting occurs between markets and even between continents. **Exhibit 5** shows car production by country. Although China and the United States are, again, the world's largest markets, the United States produces well short of its local demand. Also noticeable is that the next two countries in the ranking, Japan and Germany, produce well in excess of their domestic car demand; their surplus is exported. The reason is that these two countries are the home base of major global car manufacturers. Although car production has migrated increasingly to low-labor-cost countries in recent years, production hubs still remain in these major manufacturers' domestic countries.

Note that the total number of light vehicles in use in the world, or the total stock of light vehicles, is around 1.2 billion units. This number increases each year by the

Exhibit 5. Light Vehicle Production by Country, 2014

Country	Units (millions)
China	22.7
United States	11.7
Japan	9.8
Germany	5.9
South Korea	4.5
India	3.8
Mexico	3.4
Brazil	3.1
Spain	2.4
Canada	2.4
Russia	1.9
Thailand	1.9
France	1.8
United Kingdom	1.6
Indonesia	1.3
Czech Republic	1.3
Turkey	1.2
Iran	1.1

Source: International Organization of Motor Vehicle Manufacturers, "2014 Production Statistics" (www.oica.net/category/production-statistics).

number of new car sales minus the number of cars sent for scrappage, estimated at about 40 million units. **Exhibit 6** shows that three major regions account for a large number of vehicles in use: North America, Europe, and Asia. This figure is obviously highest in large markets where car sales have been high for a long time; the emerging markets of Latin America and Africa, relatively new to the car, have a low number of total vehicles in use. The largest individual markets for cars in use in 2013 are the United States (253 million units), China (127 million), and Japan (77 million).

Exhibit 6. Global Light Vehicles in Use, 2013

Region	Units (millions)
Europe	370
NAFTA countries	310
Central and South America	82
Asia/Oceania/Middle East	380
Africa	40

Note: NAFTA is the North American Free Trade Agreement.
Source: International Organization of Motor Vehicle Manufacturers, "Motorization Rate 2013—Worldwide" (www.oica.net/category/vehicles-in-use).

DETERMINANTS OF AUTOMOTIVE DEMAND

Demand for passenger cars is ultimately based on the desire for individual mobility, but usually demand is positively correlated with the following economic indicators, which measure consumer financial well-being:

- changes in real personal disposable income,
- house price changes,
- unemployment rate/employment, and
- consumer confidence.

Exhibit 7 shows the correlation in the US market between GDP growth and real spending on motor vehicles and parts. The "early cycle" nature of the automotive industry can be clearly seen; for example, motor vehicle demand tends to slow ahead of a GDP growth slowdown (mid-1990s, 2000, and early 2008 collapse) and reaccelerate before GDP growth reaccelerates (early 2009 recovery). The R^2 between real motor vehicle and parts spending, on the one hand, and real GDP, on the other hand, is 0.58 for this period.

Exhibit 8 shows the correlation between increases in US house prices, measured by the nationwide S&P/Case–Shiller Home Price Index, and the real growth of

Exhibit 7. Correlation between Growth in US Motor Vehicle Demand and US GDP Growth, 1994–2014

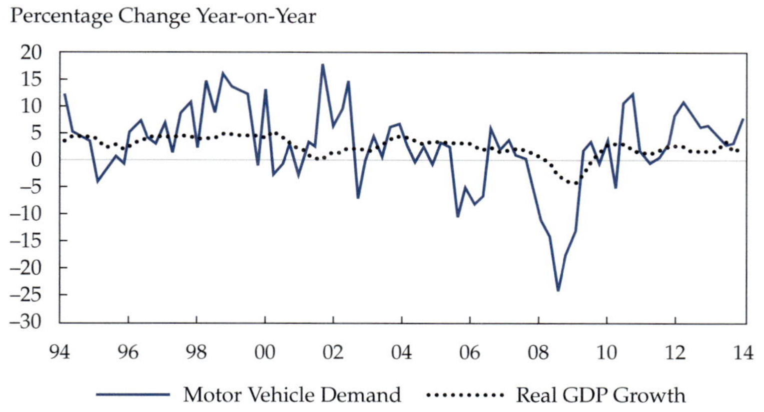

Note: Year-on-year growth rates are shown, measured each quarter.
Source: US Department of Commerce, Bureau of Economic Analysis (www.bea.gov).

Exhibit 8. Correlation between US Motor Vehicle Demand and US House Prices

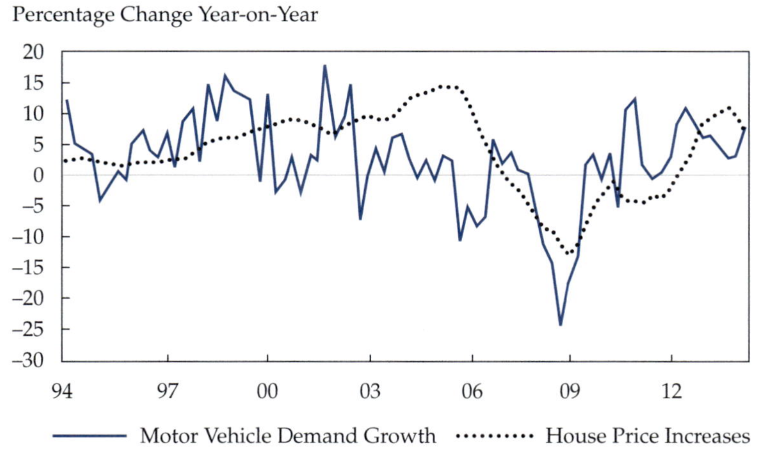

Note: Year-on-year growth rates are shown, measured each quarter.
Sources: US Department of Commerce, Bureau of Economic Analysis (www.bea.gov); S&P/Case–Shiller Home Price Index (http://us.spindices.com).

spending on motor vehicles and parts. The R^2 between real motor vehicle and parts spending and US house prices is 0.57 for this period.

The United States is a mature market as defined by car ownership per household, although that indicator has begun to decline in recent years, as shown in **Exhibit 9**. Car manufacturers see the cause as a reduced level of ownership among the population of young adults. For instance, a 25-year-old today is less likely to own a car than a 25-year-old some 30 years ago. The reasons include prolonged periods of higher education, higher youth unemployment, delayed entry into the labor force, and competition from other consumer products for young peoples' wallets.

Exhibit 9. US Car Ownership per Household, 1950–2012

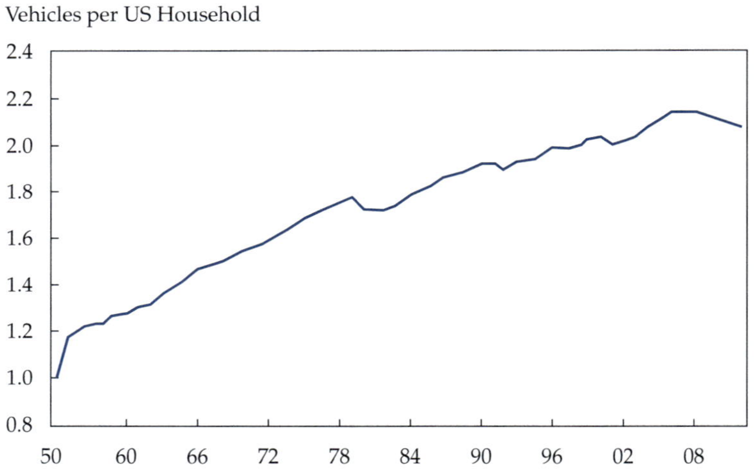

Source: US Department of Energy, Oak Ridge National Laboratory, Transportation Energy Data Book (http://cta.ornl.gov/data/chapter8.shtml).

Stagnant demand in the mature, developed economies is expected in the future. In North America, Europe, and Japan, car demand is growing only in cyclical upturns and then offset by declining demand in cyclical downturns. Car demand in these markets is essentially replacement demand, with only a small proportion of sales being first-time purchases.

Exhibit 10 shows that car ownership density is correlated with income levels, denoted by GDP per capita, and that most developed countries see a flattening out of this ownership density at GDP per capita income levels of USD30,000 or more.

Exhibit 10. Car Ownership Density and GDP per Capita by Country

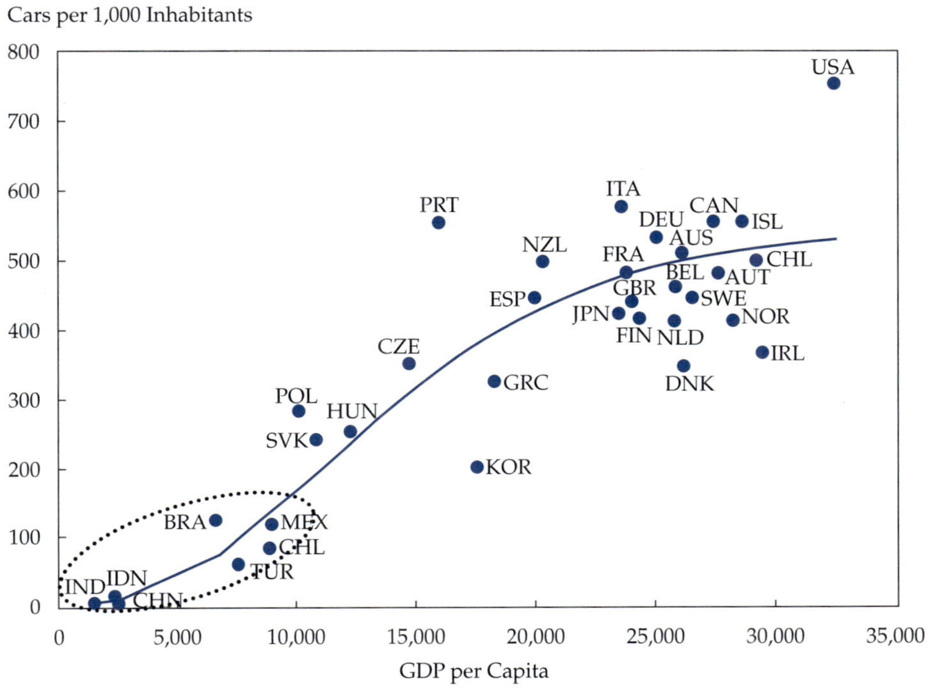

Note: GDP is measured in 1995 US dollars, purchasing power parity adjusted.
Source: OECD, "The Automobile Industry in and Beyond the Crisis" (www.oecd.org/economy/outlook/44089863.pdf).

EMERGING MARKET CAR DEMAND

The picture in emerging markets is very different. Rising middle-class incomes are creating additional spending power and enabling many households to purchase their first cars, a product once reserved for the wealthy. The income level that causes car demand to become generalized in an economy and transforms the car into a mass-market product is USD10,000 of GDP per capita in terms of US purchasing power.

The growth in car demand in emerging markets has been phenomenal, especially in China, which is now the world's largest car market after overtaking the US market in 2009. Some 43% of the increase in global car demand in volume terms over 2009–2014 is attributable to increased demand in China alone. Indeed, that market doubled in size between 2008 and 2010, years that were marked for many developed countries by the effects of the global financial crisis.

Emerging markets account for approximately 54% of global car sales in volume terms, and their significance to global demand is reflected in all auto manufacturers' plans and marketing strategies. Furthermore, this emerging market growth is expected to continue for a long time and to be the driving force of car demand worldwide.

Exhibit 11 shows the share in geographical regions of growth in car demand in volume terms for 2009–2014, the period of global economic recovery since the financial crisis. This growth has primarily been driven by emerging market demand. The North American Free Trade Agreement (NAFTA) was also a strong contributor because, although the US market fell to extreme lows in 2009, it has since strongly rebounded.

Exhibit 11. Share of Growth in Global Car Demand by Region, 2009–2014

Region	Share
Asia/Oceania/Middle East	63%
NAFTA countries	31
Central and South America	4
Russia, Turkey, and other Europe	5
Africa	2
Europe 28 and EFTA	–5

Notes: Other Europe refers to Albania, Armenia, Belarus, Bosnia, Georgia, Macedonia, Moldavia, Serbia, and Ukraine. Europe 28 is the 28 countries of the European Union, and EFTA is the European Free Trade Association.
Source: International Organization of Motor Vehicle Manufacturers (www.oica.net).

The dominance of China can be seen in **Exhibit 12**. It represented, by far, the largest emerging market for car sales in 2013. China is also 26% of global car sales. The other three of the four BRIC nations (Brazil, Russia, India, and China) pale into insignificance by comparison. A 10% growth of the Chinese market, amounting to 2.4 million units, will add 2.7% to the global growth rate of car sales.

Government policies have largely encouraged and accommodated the emergence of the motorized consumer in developing countries. Such policies include improvements and additions to road infrastructure, incentives for plant setup, and car buyer incentives. Growing urbanization, as people move away from the agrarian sector to take up employment in manufacturing and services, has also contributed to demand growth in developing markets.

Certain country idiosyncrasies, however, have brought about some special situations:

- China has been the overall success story. Strong growth in car demand took 2014 car sales to 23.5 million units, resulting in an estimated 144 million light vehicles on the road. Government and infrastructure have been accommodating, and economic growth has been supportive by slowing only moderately. In recent years, China has remained one of the world's fastest-growing emerging markets, with far stronger economic growth than its emerging market rivals.

- India is a market that has yet to emerge. Car sales are barely more than 3 million units for a population of 1.2 billion, and there are only 27 million cars on the road. A slowing economy in recent times, coupled with shifts in taxation between diesel and gasoline cars and an infrastructure that is not accommodating, has meant that India remains a small market. Urbanization is also relatively low in this country.
- More recently, Brazil has been a volatile market. Government stimulus measures have been introduced for the automobile industry, only to be sometimes swiftly withdrawn. Weak economic growth has also acted as a hindrance to demand. Given years of concern about security, the high-end market is only now starting to emerge as a significant subsegment of the market.
- Russia has been the most volatile of the emerging markets, which reflects the sensitivity of the economy to oil prices and foreign economic sanctions. Car sales dropped by 50% year-on-year in 2009, but thereafter, the market suddenly recovered, with sales nearly doubling by 2012 to just short of their 2008 peak. Car sales have slipped somewhat since then, with sales declining to close to the 2.5 million unit level with about 45 million cars on the road.

Exhibit 12. Emerging Market Car Sales, 2014

Country	Units (millions)
China	23.49
Brazil	3.50
India	3.18
Russia	2.55
Iran	1.29
Indonesia	1.21
Mexico	1.18
Thailand	0.89
Turkey	0.87
Saudi Arabia	0.83
Malaysia	0.67
South Africa	0.64
Argentina	0.61

Source: International Organization of Motor Vehicle Manufacturers, "2005–2014 Sales Statistics" (www.oica.net/category/sales-statistics).

Much of the future growth in emerging markets is expected to come from the non-BRIC countries, especially Indonesia, Thailand, Turkey, Egypt, South Africa, Argentina, Mexico, and Peru. Typically, annual car sales in these markets are a million units or less, but they could grow by 20% or so annually. Some markets, depending on how low their current sales base is, could grow even faster. In all likelihood, growth from these second-tier emerging countries as a group will outstrip growth of the market in China.

Exhibit 13 highlights 2013 motorization rates, defined as vehicles in use per 1,000 members of a population. An examination of the rates for each of the

Exhibit 13. Motorization Rates, 2013

Country	Vehicles per 1,000 People
Developed markets	
United States	790
Australia	722
New Zealand	661
Canada	635
Japan	603
Europe 28 + EFTA	564
Emerging markets	
Malaysia	397
South Korea	394
Taiwan	312
Russia	308
Argentina	301
Mexico	285
Thailand	208
Ukraine	204
Brazil	198
Turkey	182
South Africa	180
China	91
Indonesia	77
Egypt	61
Nigeria	20
India	20

Note: Europe 28 is the 28 countries of the EU, and EFTA is the European Free Trade Association.
Source: International Organization of Motor Vehicle Manufacturers (www.oica.net).

individual countries in the developing world, although the absolute number of vehicles has reached a significant level, indicates that ownership rates are still low on a per person basis. These developing markets will experience the greatest increase in car demand.

Global car demand is expected to increase in volume terms at a compound annual growth rate (CAGR) of 4%–5% in coming years. The automobile industry is often thought of as a declining one, but this global growth rate confirms that the industry is growing. Nearly all of this growth will come from developing countries because of their lower car ownership rates and faster economic growth than the developed world, rising consumer aspirations, increasing urbanization of populations, and significant infrastructure improvements.

Exhibit 14 shows that the CAGR of emerging market car demand is expected to be more than 7% through 2020, a respectable growth rate even if lower than the 10% achieved over 2000–2013. Clearly, however, no analysis of car demand is complete without a thorough understanding and analysis of emerging market demand.

Exhibit 14. Emerging vs. Developed Markets: Historical and Expected Annual Volume Sales (millions of units)

Year	Developed Markets	Emerging Markets
2000	43.3	12.9
2013	37.0	46.1
2020	42.9	75.0

Note: Emerging markets' 2000–2013 CAGR = 10.3%; 2013–2020 CAGR = 7.2%.
Source: KPMG, "Global Automotive Retail Market: From Selling Cars on the Spot to Centrally Managing the Retail Grid" (September 2013): www.kpmg.com/Global/en/IssuesAndInsights/ArticlesPublications/Documents/global-automotive-retail-market-study-part1.pdf.

Exhibit 15 graphically shows the dependence of the industry on emerging market growth in sales. The gap is widening between the growth markets of Asia and South America and the stagnant markets of Europe and North America.

CAR MANUFACTURING COMPETITIVE LANDSCAPE

Car manufacturing is a highly competitive industry. **Exhibit 16** highlights global car production by company. Of this large number of competing global and regional

Exhibit 15. Auto Industry Historical and Expected Demand by Geographical Area

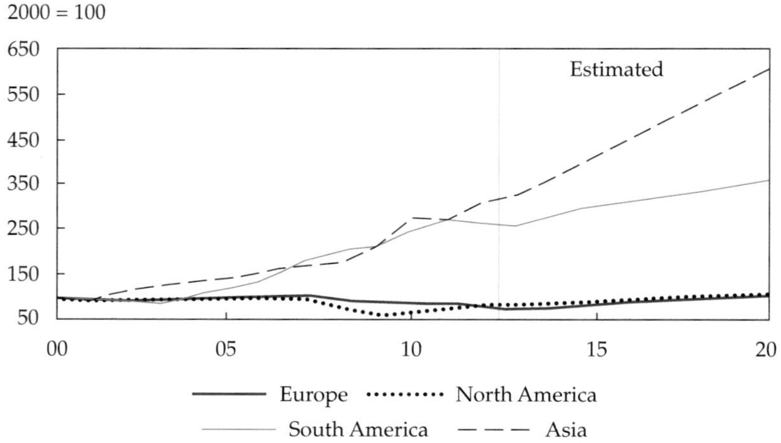

Note: Measured as domestic sales of passenger cars.
Source: OECD, "Medium-Run Capacity Adjustment in the Automobile Industry," *OECD Economics Department Policy Notes,* no. 21 (November 2013): www.oecd.org/eco/Policy%20 note_automobile.pdf.

Exhibit 16. Global Light Vehicle Production by Company, 2014

Company	Units (millions)
Toyota	10.32
General Motors	9.63
Volkswagen	9.38
Hyundai	6.91
Ford	6.08
Nissan	4.95
Fiat-Chrysler	4.68
Honda	4.30
Suzuki	2.84
Peugeot	2.83
Renault	2.70
BMW	2.01
SAIC	1.99
Daimler	1.78

Source: Based on data from www.1reservoir.com.

players, none has a commanding market share. Automotive manufacturing is thus a fragmented industry compared with some other industrial or manufacturing sectors. The top three manufacturers account for only one-third of global production, after which the size of the remaining companies drops away rather sharply. Competition among the various players is intense.

Exhibit 17 indicates the absence of pricing power in the car manufacturing industry. Price is a key factor in the consumer's purchasing decision. The long-term trend in the industry is more car for the same price or else lower prices for the same car. Manufacturers are spending more on content produced by suppliers to go into cars, but they are largely unable to raise prices to compensate for this spending because the increased functionality in content has become expected by the consumer.

The Bureau of Labor Statistics data shown in Exhibit 17 have been adjusted to take account of the increase in quality of new cars from 1990 to 2013, so the lack of pricing power is pronounced.

Car manufacturers can be sorted into two categories: mass market and premium. The mass market is where the bulk of volume occurs. Cars vary in price from low to average in this segment, and the number of players is large, so margins are low. The mass market has almost no pricing power.

In the premium and luxury segment, which includes cars in the upper segment of the market in terms of price, manufacturers have more pricing power because players are fewer and they are selling to a wealthier customer for whom the purchase is motivated by prestige, functionality of the car, and status.

Exhibit 17. US Consumer Price Index for All Items vs. New Cars

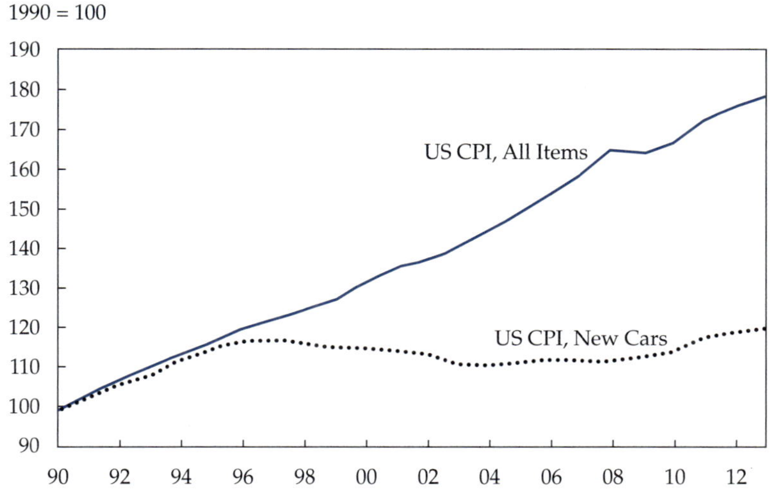

Source: US Bureau of Labor Statistics.

As shown in **Exhibit 18**, about 10% of global car sales (that is, a global average of 10%) are in the premium segment, and this segment has its highest penetration in European countries. As can be expected, premium penetration in emerging markets is currently low, providing opportunity for future growth.

Exhibit 18. Premium Segment Sales by Country Market

Country	Percent
Germany	30.0
United Kingdom	25.1
Italy	20.6
France	12.5
United States	11.8
South Korea	11.3
Turkey	11.2
Russia	8.3
China	7.9
Japan	5.8
Brazil	4.5
India	2.7

Source: BMW Group, "Investor Presentation" (June 2015): www.bmwgroup.com/d/0_0_www_bmwgroup_com/investor_relations/_pdf/2015/InvestorPresent_June_2015.pdf.

Exhibit 19 highlights selected car EBIT (earnings before interest and taxes) margins for a number of OEMs. Care has been taken to show only the car manufacturing margin, not the group consolidated EBIT margin, which usually includes a finance/leasing division and, in some cases, trucks (Volkswagen, Daimler) or motorbikes (Honda, BMW).

The mass-market players, with the exception of some of the Asian players, had low margins (in the low single digits) in 2014. Toyota benefited from a protracted period of significant cost savings. It also benefited disproportionately from the yen's weakness because it is the largest of the Japanese car exporters. Hyundai owes its high margins to efficient production techniques—a significant use of platform manufacturing strategies (in which a common plant platform is used to manufacture whole ranges of different models) and cheap parts from its *chaebol* component manufacturers (i.e., components supplied by a network of companies with interconnecting cross-shareholdings). Hyundai also has had the ability to raise car prices because a perceived quality gap between it and its competitors has narrowed. In

Exhibit 19. 2014 Car EBIT Margins by Manufacturer/Brand

Manufacturer/Brand	EBIT (%)
Peugeot	0.2
General Motors	0.5
Renault	2.2
Volkswagen brand	2.5
Honda[a]	2.8
Ford	2.9
Fiat-Chrysler[c]	3.4
Nissan[a]	3.5
Mercedes-Benz	8.0
Hyundai	8.0
Toyota[a]	9.3
BMW[b]	9.6
Audi	9.6
Maserati	9.9
Ferrari	14.1
Porsche brand	15.8

[a]Year to end March 2014.
[b]BMW includes the MINI and Rolls-Royce brands.
[c]Fiat-Chrysler includes the company's nonluxury brands.
Source: Company websites.

general, rarely can a mass-market manufacturer sustain an EBIT margin of 3%, and it can experience regular periods of losses, particularly among manufacturers with a high European exposure.

Categorizing companies in this standardized manner is difficult, however, because such mass-market players as Peugeot and Renault have models that compete with the lower end of the premium market. So, there is some overlap in competitive terms. The Japanese manufacturers have premium models as well. For example, Lexus is the Toyota group's premium model, and Acura and Infiniti are the premium models of Honda and Nissan, respectively. These cars in the premium segment make only a small unit contribution to these companies' sales.

The premium segment's margins are clearly significantly higher than those in the mass market. These margins regularly reach low double digits in good years and are profitable even in recession years. Luxury brands carry the highest margins, often in the 15%–20% range.

The industry rule of thumb is that car manufacturing margins are proportional to the car's size: Smaller cars are more likely to belong to the mass market and have lower margins, whereas premium cars are more likely to be larger in size and carry higher margins.

The gap between mass-market and luxury margins has been sustainable long term, as **Exhibit 20** shows. Essentially, the margin difference is a result of the difference in pricing power previously discussed and of different market structures among the regions, including differences in capacity utilization.

BMW is a good example of a premium car manufacturer. It is arguably one of the highest-quality OEMs, with strong management and a conservative approach. Except in the 2008 and 2009 crisis years—when sales slumped and most OEMs generated losses, some of the losses significant—its car EBIT margin has been consistently positive. The remarkable stability of BMW's margins in profitable years, generating a margin of 6%–8% between 2000 and 2007, is especially impressive in light of the car industry's volatility and unpredictability.

In the mass market, Ford struggled with persistent losses between 2000 and 2009, much of it caused by heavy provisioning and restructuring. This period was a time of growing Japanese encroachment into the market of Detroit's "Big Three" (Ford, General Motors, and Chrysler). At that time, significant amounts of market share were lost to the Japanese companies. Weak pricing and market share loss created an unprofitable business model. Since the financial crisis of 2008–2009, when much capacity was taken out of the US market and many models were scrapped, Ford

Exhibit 20. Car EBIT Margins by Manufacturer, 2000–2013

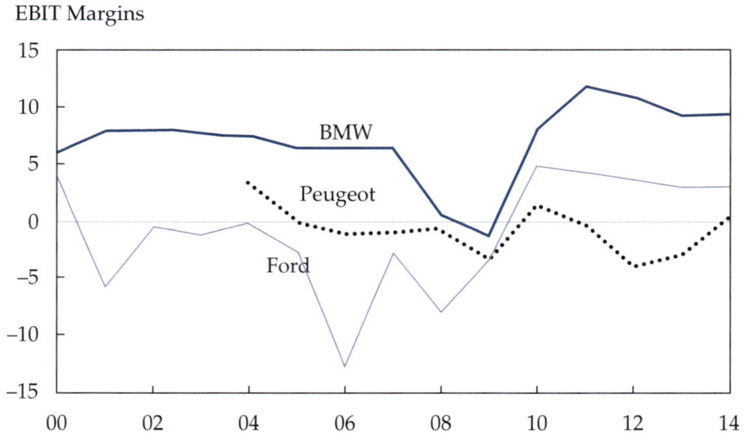

Note: BMW includes the MINI and Rolls-Royce brands.
Source: Company websites.

has made a remarkable recovery in profits. It owes its current profitability to high margins in the US market. Overall, Ford's EBIT margins remain typical of what an investor might expect a mass-market OEM to earn.

Exhibit 21 explains one reason for Ford's quick return to healthy profitability in the US market, namely, capacity exiting the US industry. The other reason is better industry discipline on pricing.

Exhibit 21. Capacity Utilization in the US Auto Industry, 2014

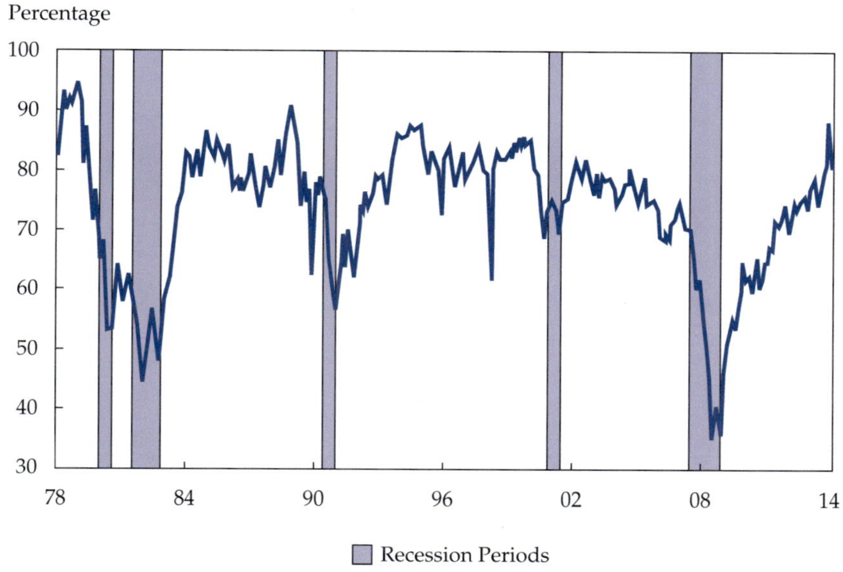

Source: Based on data from the US Federal Reserve Board, 2014.

Peugeot is a different story. Despite a growing sales exposure outside Europe, it is still highly exposed in Europe, where car sales have been falling steadily, with some recovery in 2014. Europe is a notoriously difficult market. It has intense price competition and few players making healthy margins. The reason is chronic overcapacity in the industry, as illustrated in **Exhibit 22**. Europe has more than 10 manufacturing plants considered to have excess capacity. Political pressures, the high cost of redundancies (layoffs), and union power all act to considerably slow down the necessary restructuring and inevitable job losses. No company wants to be the first to cut capacity because doing so usually means lower sales and market share.

In 2012, European capacity utilization was approximately 70%, and it fell slightly more in 2013. The usual effect of low capacity utilization in the automobile industry is low (or no) profitability, which pressures the OEMs to sell more volume. The OEMs

Exhibit 22. European Capacity Utilization in the Auto Industry, 2012 vs. 2013

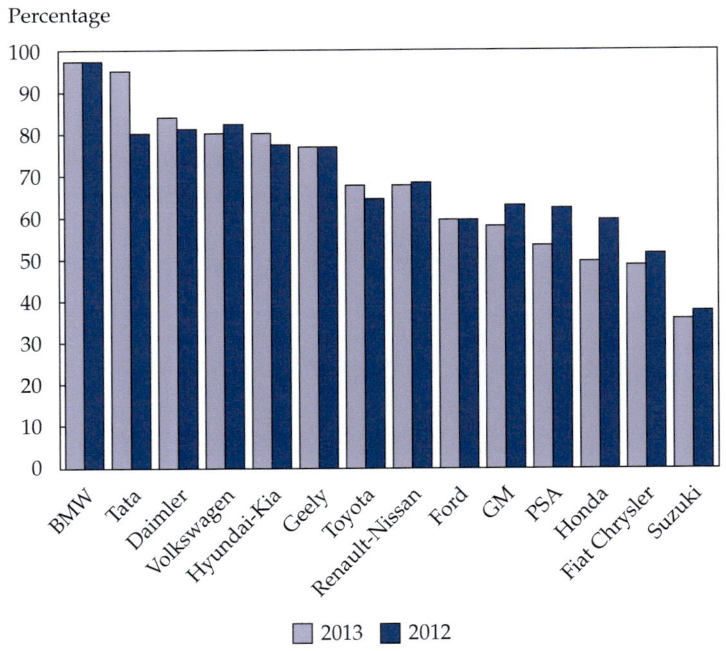

Source: Based on data from Inovev (www.inovev.com/index.php/en).

can attempt to increase volume through incentive spending, by discounting prices to dealers or encouraging dealers to discount with a contribution from the OEMs.

This subject is controversial in the automobile industry because rarely will a car manufacturer admit to discounting prices to shift volume, but that is what regularly happens. Even if discounting is not the manufacturer's strategy, it is a means of disposing of excess inventory. It often occurs when a manufacturer has an aging fleet and is disposing of old models to make way for new. The level of discounting contributes to the volatility of earnings and the overall competitive intensity in the automobile industry. That margins are low, particularly for the mass-market manufacturers, generates high earnings volatility when pricing responds to capacity utilization issues.

Although the US market is experiencing increasing volumes, **Exhibit 23** highlights that incentive spending has been trending upward since 2012. This trend is often a symptom of a market that is near its peak; that is, as growth rates slow, even though they remain positive, car manufacturers are still under pressure to sell more volume.

Exhibit 23. Incentive Spending in the US Auto Industry, 2009–First Half 2014

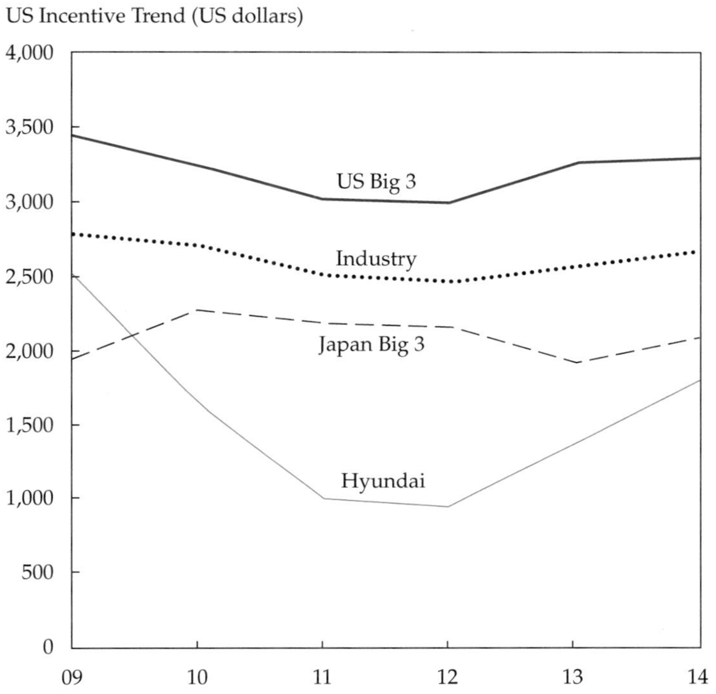

Source: Hyundai investor presentation (August 2014).

TRENDS IN THE AUTOMOBILE MANUFACTURING INDUSTRY

Some recovery in global car demand occurred in 2010–2014 following the steep fall in car sales in 2009, and 2014 was the fifth consecutive year of rising car sales volume worldwide. As shown in **Exhibit 24**, however, the increase in demand is coming mainly from China, the United States, and to a moderate degree, Europe. The general trend in nearly all emerging markets has been falling demand, so China's strength is even more impressive than in the years when the emerging markets all grew together. For some emerging markets (Brazil, Russia), the weakness that started in 2013 accelerated into 2014; for others (India), the market appears to have bottomed and is resuming growth.

Revenue and earnings results in 2014 showed similar trends among the larger OEMs: sluggish top-line growth in volume as emerging market demand declined,

Exhibit 24. Slowing Volume Growth in Emerging Markets

Market	Fiscal Year (FY) 2013	First Half 2014	FY 2014
Europe 28 + EFTA	–1.6%	6.5%	5.4%
United States	7.4	4.3	5.8
Brazil	–0.9	–7.6	–6.9
China	13.9	8.4	12.8
Japan	0.1	10.8	3.0
India	–9.9	–7.2	0.7
Russia	–6.1	–6.5	–10.3

Note: Europe 28 is the 28 countries of the European Union, and EFTA is the European Free Trade Association.
Sources: International Organization of Motor Vehicle Manufacturers and Verband der Automobilindustrie websites.

particularly in Latin America, while growth in US demand slowed slightly. The recovery in European demand was not sufficient to fully offset weakness in other areas. Coupled with this slowdown, currency devaluations, particularly arising in the emerging markets (Brazil, Russia, and India), hurt revenues. As a result, revenue growth in 2014 was generally expected to have been flat to negative.

Exhibit 25 shows that profit margins are not faring much better than income. The years 2010–2014 have generally been a time of industrywide decline in EBIT margins brought on by a number of cost pressures, notably the following:

- capacity expansion in emerging markets;
- new technologies linked to emissions control;
- new product launches;
- the development of the electric car (not offset by sales); and
- an increase in new technology and amenities in cars, the cost of which manufacturers have been unable to pass on to final consumers.

Some of these cost pressures have been offset by improved efficiency, either from direct cost cutting or from savings from the wider adoption of platform technologies and modularity. For this reason, the decline in EBIT margins during the period has been mild, with the exception of Toyota.

In general, pricing seems to be stable and is being used in emerging markets to compensate for currency devaluations, which had led to loss of market share for

Exhibit 25. EBIT Margins of Global OEMs, 2010–2014

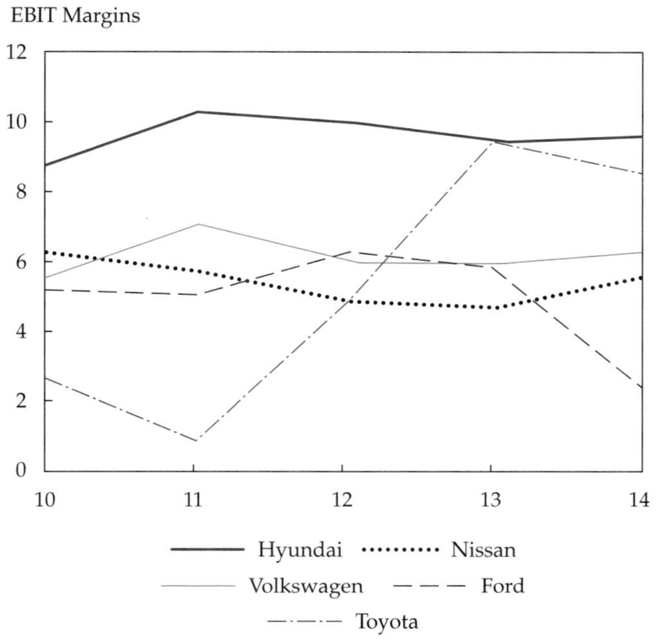

Source: Hyundai Motor Company, "Investor Presentation" (May 2015): http://worldwide.hyundai.com/wcm/idc/groups/sggeneralcontent/@hmc/documents/sitecontent/mdaw/mdk4/~edisp/hw098669.pdf.

some players that adopted this pricing strategy. In Europe, the pricing environment remains difficult, as witnessed by weak margins at some of Volkswagen's European-focused brands (the SEAT brand is continuing to lose money), by continuing low margins for Japanese operators, and by both Ford and GM slowly reducing their European losses.

Profits from leasing and financing are also stable, although margins are eroding because of higher credit provisions and lower expected residual values. The major OEMs' leasing and finance businesses remain solidly profitable.

In terms of segments by body style, **Exhibit 26** indicates a trend toward smaller cars and SUVs/crossovers (CUVs). Compact premium cars are doing well in terms of sales, and the growth of the SUV market share is seen in a number of regions, including the United States, China, and India. This has largely been at the expense of the standard sedan models.

Sales of electric vehicles—in particular, the hybrid electric car—are growing strongly but from a very low base, so sales are still only a small fraction of total car sales. Estimates for the total number of electric vehicles (including plug-in, battery, and all-electric models) on the roads worldwide are around 600,000 in 2014, with 260,000 in the United States and fewer than 100,000 units each in China and Japan.

Exhibit 26. Cumulative US Market Share by Body Style, 2009–2014

Body Style	2009	2010	2011	2012	2013	2014
SUV/CUV	31.4%	33.6%	34.4%	33.3%	33.9%	36.5%
Sedan	36.3	36.2	36.5	36.5	36.6	35.4
Pickup	14.1	13.8	12.7	12.8	13.6	13.1
Hatchback	5.6	5.0	6.2	6.6	6.0	5.5

Note: Data shown are cumulative market share to May each year.
Source: IHS Automotive data from www.thecarconnection.com.

AUTOMOTIVE COMPONENT MANUFACTURERS

INDUSTRY OVERVIEW

Generalizations about automotive component manufacturers are difficult to make because each product is distinct; indeed, each subsegment of component manufacturing should be considered individually. For example, every subsegment in this industry has a different level of industry concentration, pricing power, and growth rate, and each product has a different significance in terms of unit cost to the car manufacturer and value added for the car driver.

An important distinction is between parts manufactured for new cars and those manufactured for the aftermarket (i.e., vehicles already on the road). Manufacturing of new cars is known as original equipment (OE), as related to OEM (original equipment manufacturer).

The aftermarket includes both parts and service, which are typically replacement parts for those worn out or damaged in cars that have already been sold to consumers. These parts are the same as those manufactured for new cars and supplied to the OEMs. Typically, the same company produces parts both for OEMs and for replacement customers, usually garages or car dealership networks. Usually, the part manufacturer will split its business between these two customer channels.

Automotive component manufacturers are sometimes referred to as "car suppliers." Such suppliers are found at various places in the automotive supply chain. Some are component manufacturers supplying braking systems, wiring, steering wheels, and other components. Others are more like assemblers; they buy finished car parts and assemble them for the car manufacturers. A good example of assembly is car seats; an assembler buys the seat frame, textiles, foam, and plastics and creates a car seat that can be delivered directly to the car manufacturer.

The global components industry is estimated to have annual revenue of more than USD1.5 trillion. It is split, as shown in **Exhibit 27**, between more than USD1 trillion in original equipment and USD500 billion in aftermarket sales.

The OE estimates in Exhibit 27 are based on the value of content (i.e., technology and/or amenities) going into a new car in the developed markets of approximately USD14,500 per unit manufactured by a major OEM. In emerging markets, it was assumed that content per car is about one-third lower than in developed markets, or USD9,500 per car. The global average content per car is USD11,800. Multiplying

Exhibit 27. Annual Revenues of Global Components Manufacturing Industry, 2009 vs. 2014 (USD billions)

Market	2009	2014
Original equipment		
United States	119	229
Europe	204	236
China	123	269
Japan and South Korea	136	162
Others	113	149
Total	695	1,045
Aftermarket	375	502
Grand total	1,070	1,547

Note: Data do not include tires, discussed in the next section of this report.
Sources: Original Equipment Suppliers Association and Motor & Equipment Manufacturers Association. OE figures for 2009 are from the US Department of Commerce, "On the Road: U.S. Automotive Parts Industry Annual Assessment" (2011): www.trade.gov/static/2011Parts.pdf. The 2014 OE estimates and both aftermarket estimates are the author's.

that figure by the 89 million global units produced in 2014 produces USD1.05 trillion, equivalent to the estimate in Exhibit 27.

The aftermarket estimate in Exhibit 27 was derived from applying a long-term 6% growth rate to the 2009 market estimate of USD375 billion provided by the US Department of Commerce. This growth rate breaks down into a 3% increase in the number of light vehicles on the roads globally and 3% volume growth from an aging fleet, with pricing flat. Intuitively, the aftermarket is usually around 50% of the size of the OE market.

Exhibit 28 highlights the fragmented nature of the global component manufacturing industry. The top 10 manufacturers account for less than 20% of industry revenues.

In terms of original equipment manufacturing, from a definitional perspective, component suppliers are classified into tiers:

- first tier—supplying the OEMs directly,
- second tier—supplying first-tier suppliers,
- third tier—lower still, and so on down the supply chain.

An example of a second-tier supplier is a manufacturer of carbon black, which is used in tire manufacturing, or of copper wire. The carbon black supplier is a

Exhibit 28. Top 10 Global Automotive Component Manufacturers, 2012

Rank	Company	2012 Revenues (USD millions)
1	Robert Bosch	36,787
2	Denso	34,200
3	Continental	32,800
4	Magna	30,428
5	Aisin Seiki	30,080
6	Johnson Controls	22,515
7	Faurecia	22,500
8	Hyundai Mobis	21,351
9	ZF Friedrichshafen	18,614
10	Yazaki	15,801

Source: "Top Suppliers: North America, Europe and the World," *Automotive News*, Supplement (17 June 2013): www.autonews.com/assets/pdf/CA89220617.PDF.

second-tier supplier in the supply chain, whereas the tire manufacturer is a first-tier supplier selling directly to the OEMs. The manufacturer of copper wire is a second-tier supplier to the wiring system manufacturer, which is a first-tier supplier to a car manufacturer. These relationships are illustrated in **Exhibit 29**.

Nearly all the major component manufacturers listed in Exhibit 28 are first-tier suppliers, although some lower-tier suppliers are also listed. The lower in the supply chain, the smaller the companies become and, usually, the more fragmented the market is in terms of the number of companies operating in that space. The lower end of the supply chain is also where value added is lowest; the products manufactured tend to resemble a commodity and are highly labor intensive.

DETERMINANTS OF DEMAND FOR AUTOMOTIVE COMPONENTS

Essentially, demand for components is determined by OEMs' production schedules, so growth or contraction in the volume of car manufacturing leads directly to growth or contraction in component manufacturing. Component manufacturers do not want inventory levels to fluctuate wildly as a function of car production, so they tailor their own component manufacturing to car production schedules.

Government regulations on safety and fuel economy, with some equipment specifically mandated, are key drivers of component manufacturers' revenues. For example,

Exhibit 29. Illustration of the Tier Structure of Automotive Component Manufacturers

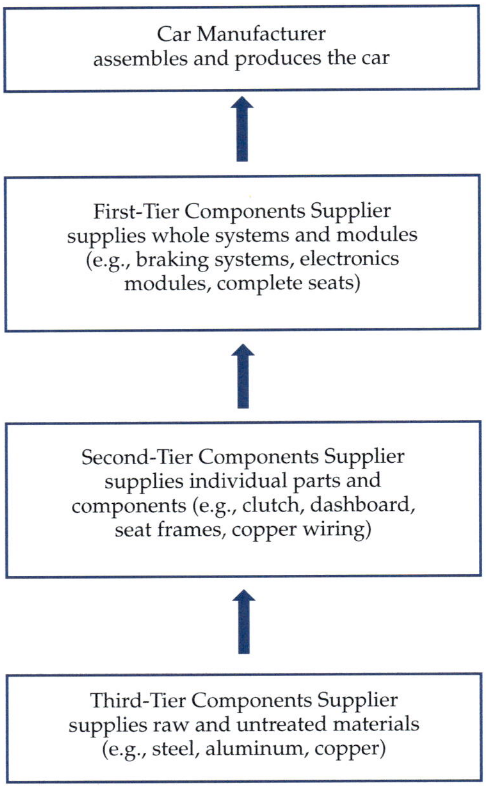

rear-view cameras in the United States are being phased in beginning in May 2016 and will be mandatory in all new vehicles manufactured from 2018. A similar pattern was followed for safety legislation involving seat belts and passenger airbags in past decades. Emissions control (to decrease emissions of carbon dioxide, CO_2) is another aspect that governments worldwide have legislated and that has had a direct impact on OEMs and their suppliers. Electronic stability control systems have been mandatory since 2012 in Europe and North America.

Emerging economies are also following the trend of increased government regulation, which stimulates strong growth in certain segments of the component industry.

Content per car in terms of original equipment is estimated to be growing by 2%–3% annually. In theory, volume growth for component manufacturers should be greater than the volume growth of car production or the volume growth of their OEM customers, and this growth is regularly borne out when suppliers publish their quarterly or half-yearly earnings reports. This trend is aside from the trend, discussed later in this section, of OEMs choosing the more global suppliers at the expense of more local or regional ones. In this case, the favored suppliers' higher volume growth is partly explained by market share gain.

The degree of outsourcing by OEMs can also influence a supplier's growth rate, but a clear trend cannot be determined. For example, Volkswagen still manufactures most components in-house and subcontracts relatively little to suppliers compared with other OEMs. Volume growth of car manufacturing does not necessarily lead to increased outsourcing of component manufacturing.

COMPONENT SUPPLIER CONTRACTS WITH OEMS

Component manufacturers are hired by OEMs to fulfill the product requirements of a particular model. Generally, they do not supply an OEM with parts for all its models. For example, when the Audi A3 is revamped, parent company Volkswagen will put out a tender for the contract for parts for the Audi A3 only. Usually, the car manufacturer will have more than one supplier of a particular product, in case the main supplier has logistical issues or some other type of impediment to its ability to deliver the components on time.

Generally, the supplier bids for the full life of a car model cycle, which is generally about seven years. The first two years, however, are the design stage, so before the car goes into production, the component manufacturer will work with the OEM on the design of the car, its size, and its engine capacity to determine the particular product requirements.

The contract is often volume based, meaning that the component manufacturer is paid on a per-unit basis and can pass on to the OEM any unforeseen cost increases—for example, if steel or aluminum prices increase. This can provide some degree of insulation to the component manufacturer's margins. Thus, the component manufacturer's business is volume sensitive, and these companies share in the fortunes of an OEM's new product launch (assuming a successful model launch).

The OEM generally awards contracts based on the following supplier characteristics:

- technology content,
- cost and efficiency,
- reliability and logistics,
- global reach, and
- flexibility in adjusting to changed circumstances.

Contracts have low profit visibility because the OEM usually knows the production schedule only for the next three months. Thereafter, volumes can vary on the basis of a particular plant's production requirements, which in turn depend on the sales success of the models that plant is producing. The component manufacturer assumes contract-related risk in terms of both how much volume it will supply and the length of the production horizon. Neither term can be foreseen with any degree of certainty.

After the car's initial launch, the component manufacturer is usually still under contract for another five years. Each year, the contracts have price reductions—or, in industry terminology, "price downs"—that are agreed on at the start of the contract. These price reductions are usually in the 2%–3% range but can vary depending on the particular product, the relationship between OEM and supplier, perceived pricing power, and degree of industry consolidation in the manufacture of that particular component. Often, the component manufacturer will take into account the likely annual price reductions when pricing the contract; it is a standard practice in the automotive supplier industry.

These price reductions can be renegotiated at the end of each year, and in the case of disagreement, a component manufacturer and an OEM can part ways at that point. To a certain degree, however, the OEM is a captive customer, because it would have to switch to another supplier in the middle years of a product launch and that supplier might turn out to be more expensive and/or less reliable than the original one.

Price is far from the most important aspect of a contract between supplier and OEM. Without parts—for example, if a logistics problem with a component supplier occurred—sales would be adversely affected. This loss in sales would then tie up the OEM's working capital, causing a cash flow issue. As a result, suppliers often locate their plants close to their OEM customer's plants. This strategy allows them to respond promptly to last-minute requests and also provides flexibility in their own production.

A further dimension is that the large OEMs are now international. They have been awarding more global contracts and preferring suppliers that can accommodate them globally. Typically, cars are launched in one geographical zone, followed by launches in other zones at staged intervals, making a global launch manageable. OEMs have been dropping small, regional suppliers in favor of global ones, thereby making the capacity to deliver on a global scale a key factor in awarding contracts.

THE AFTERMARKET

The factors that determine and influence sales in the aftermarket include the following:

- number and age of vehicles in use,
- amount of delayed maintenance from previous periods, and
- fuel costs.

The first two factors are positive for the aftermarket: An aging vehicle fleet increases repairs and maintenance. The older a car is, the more repairs are usually required to maintain it in a suitable state of operation. Also, customers can wait only so long if they choose to delay a particular repair, so demand usually recovers rapidly. Fuel costs inhibit aftermarket demand because high fuel costs encourage scrappage and the replacement of a vehicle with one that is more fuel efficient.

Exhibit 30 shows that the average age of the light vehicle fleet in the United States has been increasing in recent years. Sales have been lower than trend despite the recovery since the 2009 crisis year. This factor is positive for aftermarket sales.

In Europe, the average fleet age is 8.6 years, much younger than in the United States, because of the extent and scale of the scrappage schemes undertaken there in 2009 and 2010 to counteract the global recession. The average age in Europe is increasing now, however, because the impact of the scrappage schemes gave a one-off boost to sales that caused a significant drop in the average age of the vehicle fleet. The scrappage scheme in the United States (Cash for Clunkers) was only one month long (August 2009).

In developing markets, the average fleet age is usually very low (the estimate is five years in China) because most cars have been purchased in the last few years. Correspondingly, the aftermarket is small and undeveloped. Strong growth in car sales in these developing markets should eventually lead to an aging fleet and significant growth in the aftermarket, especially as first-time drivers develop the habit of taking care of their cars.

Aftermarket demand is a function of the number of light vehicles in use, which is around 1.2 billion worldwide. This figure is growing by around 40 million vehicles, or 3%, annually. Growth of the aftermarket in volume terms should be faster than this rate in light of the worldwide aging of the fleet.

Exhibit 30. Average Age of US Light Vehicles, 2002–2013

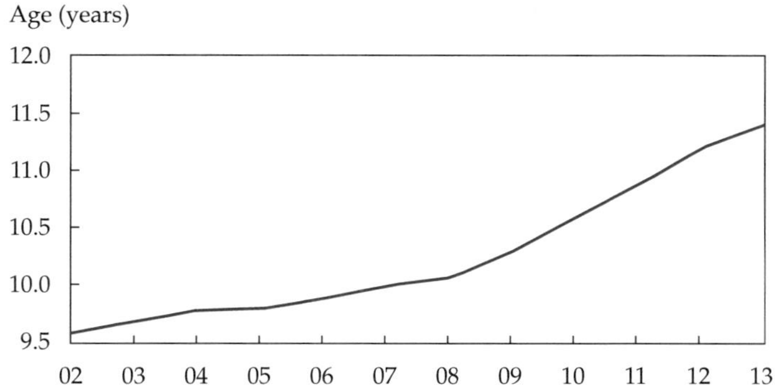

Source: Polk (August 2013).

AUTOMOTIVE COMPONENT COMPETITIVE LANDSCAPE

ABSENCE OF PRICING POWER

In general, apart from a few specific instances, component suppliers do not have much pricing power. The number of suppliers per product is usually sufficient to maintain competitive pressures, although some particular product segments are quite consolidated. Overall, each product going into a car needs to be analyzed individually as to the number of potential suppliers and how consolidated that product segment is.

Components have various degrees of importance to the consumer. Basically, anything that the driver cannot see, usually contained in the frame of the car, is not considered important enough to differentiate for the component manufacturer; that is, such components, in the opinion of the car manufacturers, have little or no pricing power. Otherwise, the supplier and OEM would be able to pass on the cost, or cost increases, to the end consumer. In addition, some components are so standardized that they are not important to consumers' purchasing decisions. Examples are car doors, steering wheels, and hand brakes. Typically, the car purchaser is prepared to pay for the following:

- Improved fuel economy because it provides a financial benefit
- Safety features, which have become a priority, and some of which are the subject of government legislation and regulation
- "Infotainment" because drivers are demanding improved entertainment and connectivity with the outside world
- Increased comfort and convenience

Pricing power is a function of the structure of the industry in that supplier's business segment. If a supplier has a commanding position in a particular product segment, even in the production of a commoditized product, sometimes that supplier has pricing power, in which case the EBIT margin can be significant. Much depends on where the product fits into the value chain for the OEM, how much more salable the product is likely to render the car, and whether the cost of the product can be passed on to the final consumer.

The reverse can also be true: Margins can be low in a high-value-added but fragmented segment because of competitive pressures from other players. For example, years of intense competition in the highly fragmented car interiors business (dashboards, floor frames) have led to chronically low margins and often losses. As a result, many players are attempting to exit this industry segment.

Investors familiar with the automotive industry tend to assume that suppliers usually suffer at the hands of their OEM customers and get squeezed by them in hard times. The assumption is that contracts are set up in such a way that OEMs place increased pricing pressure on their suppliers in order to protect their own margins. OEMs do have some bargaining power and have been known to negotiate vigorously on contract pricing, often asking suppliers to give better (lower) pricing. The reality is more sophisticated, however, than this casual analysis suggests. There is a growing interdependence between the suppliers and OEMs. Price is becoming less crucial to the contract decision than other parameters; logistics, technology, global reach, product quality, and reliability have become increasingly important. Today, an OEM is likely to be primarily concerned about which supplier can support its global growth by supplying parts to its plants worldwide. The concern with price has become only one parameter in a complex and interdependent relationship.

Exhibit 31 highlights the margin hierarchy in component manufacturing. Suppliers involved mainly in component assembly, such as French-listed Faurecia, generate the lowest margins—often mid-single-digit EBIT margins or below. Next are the low-value-added component manufacturers, such as Canadian-listed Magna, whose EBIT margins are usually in the 5%–10% range, depending on the specific product, cost structure, and efficiency. The highest margins are generated from high-value-added products, such as those linked to fuel economy or emissions control (e.g.,

Exhibit 31. Margin Hierarchy in Component Manufacturing

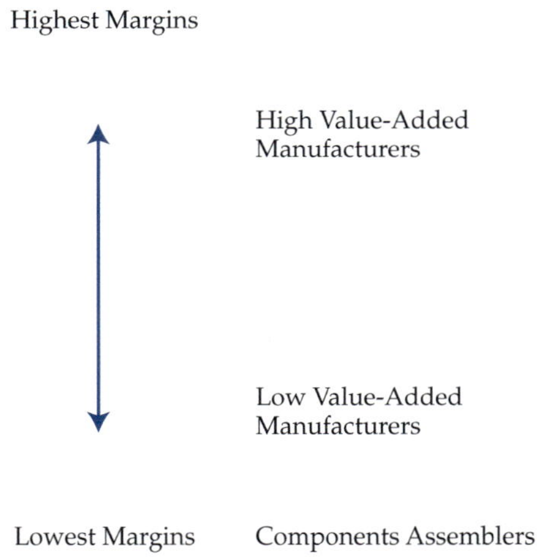

turbochargers from BorgWarner and safety, detection, and warning devices from Continental), which can typically achieve EBIT margins in double digits.

Exhibit 32 shows the trend from 2005 to 2014 in the automotive supplier industry's average EBIT margin, after restructuring charges. Aside from the crisis years of 2008 and 2009, the industry average EBIT margin has typically been between 6% and 7% in the decade ending in 2014.

Exhibit 32. Average Automotive Component Supplier EBIT Margin, 2005–2014 Estimate

Year	EBIT Margin
2005	6.0%
2006	5.7
2007	6.5
2008	2.1
2009	1.8
2010	7.0
2011	6.5
2012	6.9
2013	7.2
2014 (estimate)	7.5

Note: After restructuring charges and based on a sample of 600 suppliers.
Source: Roland Berger/Lazard.

INDUSTRY STRUCTURE

Component manufacturers are sometimes linked by capital structure to OEMs, with the OEMs owning either majority or minority stakes in the suppliers. In Europe, for example, there are Fiat-Chrysler with its 100%-owned subsidiary Magneti Marelli and Peugeot with its majority-controlled subsidiary Faurecia. Such examples are rare in North America, however, where component manufacturers tend to be independent of OEMs.

This linking by capital structure is most apparent in Asia, where the South Korean *chaebol* and Japanese *keiretsu* organizational structures are regularly in place in the automotive industry. The meaning of *chaebol* is "business family" or "monopoly" in Korean; a *chaebol* is like an interconnecting galaxy of cross-holdings. In Japanese, the meaning of *keiretsu* is, loosely translated, "headless combine." It is a structure of one parent company owning stakes in a number of others with which it has some sort of operating affinity. Often, the stakes are in suppliers. These structures have a significant impact on the fortunes of the component manufacturers concerned, both in terms of reliance on the "parent" OEM and in terms of the suppliers' abilities to successfully pursue global growth.

By developing a close web of cross-shareholdings and stakes, the South Korean *chaebol* and Japanese *keiretsu* aim to foster a trusting relationship, close cooperation, and improved sharing of knowledge and information between suppliers and OEMs. Theoretically, the result should be a better-quality and more cheaply produced product. The structures enable OEMs to benefit from a dedicated network of nearly exclusive suppliers. They also enhance control over the development of new technology while maintaining an element of confidentiality and secrecy. The component manufacturers often generate the bulk of their business with their *keiretsu* or *chaebol* partners, and their remaining business is spread across a large number of competitor OEMs, so each non-*keiretsu* OEM's individual business is often marginal.

Exhibit 33 highlights the heavy dependence of Toyota's component manufacturers on the parent company, Toyota. The main detriment is that Toyota is both the main shareholder and main customer, so its demand is the priority for the component manufacturer irrespective of the profitability of any particular contract.

Much the same could be said of Honda and its component suppliers, which also operate within a *keiretsu* structure. Only Nissan has taken significant steps to dismantle its *keiretsu* by putting contracts up for global bidding, diversifying its supplier base, and awarding more contracts to foreign and non-*keiretsu* component manufacturers.

The main disadvantages of the *keiretsu* system are as follows:

- The component manufacturer's main objective is to service the parent; it usually does not aggressively pursue global growth or win significant new business with non-*keiretsu* OEMs.

Exhibit 33. Toyota's Stake in Component Manufacturers, 2013

Supplier	2013 Global Rank	Toyota's Stake	Toyota's Global Share of Sales
Denso	2	22%	49%
Aisin Seiki	5	23	64
Toyota Boshoku	18	39	32
Toyoda Gosei	23	43	28

Source: Hans Greimel, "Japan's Keiretsu Suppliers at Risk in a New Reality," *Automotive News* (29 September 2014).

- Overall, this structure limits suppliers' growth and makes them locally focused on high-cost Japanese production, less global, and more dependent on the parent company, thereby increasing the suppliers' operational risk and potentially limiting their profitability and future growth of earnings.
- The *keiretsu* system operates like a defensive mechanism because the parent company's stake is effectively a blocking minority. Usually, this structure protects the weak industrial players from takeovers, so it is not conducive to good management, profit maximization, or the adoption of best practices or implementation of new techniques.
- It locks the OEM into high-cost suppliers, decreasing the OEM's competitiveness because contracts are more likely to be awarded on the basis of relationships and historical links with suppliers than as a result of cost efficiency and technology.

For these reasons, in an age of globalization and competitive and flexible markets, some critics argue that the *keiretsu* system is no longer viable and does not provide the flexibility necessary for a global OEM to compete successfully.

The *chaebol* has a different capital structure. It is more complex than the *keiretsu* and involves numerous cross-holdings. A simplified version of the Hyundai/Kia/Mobis *chaebol* is shown in **Exhibit 34**.

Exhibit 34. Simple View of Hyundai/Kia/Mobis *Chaebol*

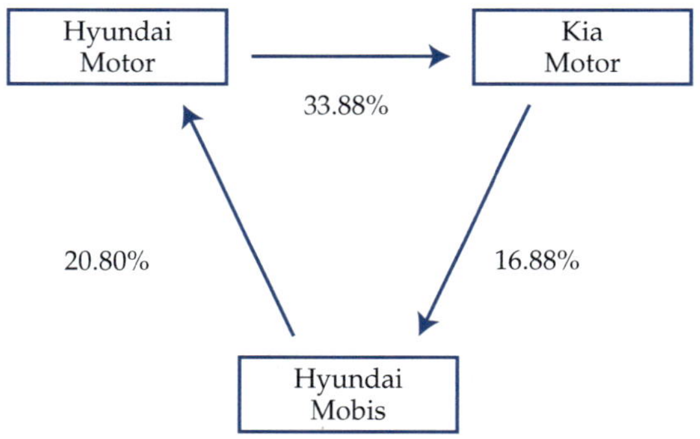

Source: Company annual reports.

Exhibit 35 shows an even greater dependence of the component manufacturer's sales on the main shareholder, particularly in the case of Hyundai Mobis.

This structure does not appear to have impeded any of the companies' performances, perhaps because of Hyundai and Kia's success at globalizing and gaining market share as well as developing an efficient operating infrastructure with

Exhibit 35. Hyundai/Kia/Mobis *Chaebol*: Sales Relationship

Supplier	Hyundai Motor's Stake	Kia Motor's Stake	Sales Dependence on Hyundai/Kia Motors
Hyundai Mobis	—	16.88%	>90%
Hyundai Wia	25.35%	13.44%	75
Mando Corp.	—	—	58

Source: 2014 company annual reports.

numerous plants in low-cost developing countries. Hyundai Mobis is greatly tied to the fortunes of two OEMs, however, and will thus depend on Hyundai and Kia's model-launch cycles and production schedules. There are no direct stakes of car manufacturers or suppliers in Mando Corporation, but the company is part of Halla Group, a South Korean industrial conglomerate and itself a *chaebol*.

The great dependence of some Asian component manufacturers on just one or two OEMs contrasts markedly with the pattern seen in other parts of the world. Component manufacturers have become more global as they have followed the globalization of the OEMs and often situate plants close to an OEM's manufacturing capacity. This practice has allowed them to obtain business from other local OEMs, bringing about a more diversified client portfolio and greater geographical exposure than before.

A North American component manufacturer will commonly have Europe as its biggest region in terms of sales. In many cases, North American sales are lower than European sales. A good example is BorgWarner, the US-listed turbocharger manufacturer, which had 50% of its 2014 sales in Europe despite being US listed and having its global headquarters in the United States.

Similarly, European suppliers have been diversifying away from Europe, where they usually have 50% of their sales at most, to the emerging markets. The result is to cause their European exposure to drop further. For example, in terms of OEM customers, Faurecia is not dependent on its parent company, Peugeot, which accounts for only 14% of its sales (Peugeot and Citroën brands together). In fact, Volkswagen, at 25% of 2014 sales, is Faurecia's biggest customer.

In summary, the component manufacturing industry is structured according to the particular business culture of the manufacturer's domestic origin. Globalization has diversified both the geographical exposure and customer sales exposure of the manufacturers and has opened up new growth opportunities. Contracts are becoming increasingly global in reach, which is one of the benchmarks against which the component manufacturers are being judged in terms of their fulfillment ability.

TRENDS IN AUTOMOTIVE COMPONENT MANUFACTURING

Component manufacturers' earnings in 2014 were generally favorable, with volumes increasing and margins slightly improving. Top-line volume growth has slowed, however, as car production schedules and launches have slowed. In addition, emerging markets and currencies have been key weaknesses. Pricing has been negative for many companies, hampering earnings growth.

Long term, the underlying demand trends for components are supported by the following:

- increased use of electronics (more wiring, more autonomous functions),
- greater connectivity (internet, phone, information systems),
- focus on fuel economy and emissions control (engine downsizing, turbochargers, stop/start functions, direct fuel injection),[2]
- active safety devices (driver assistance, detection systems, alerts, vision aids),
- growing infotainment (increased comfort levels, information, touch screens), and
- lighter cars (aluminum replacing steel, plastics replacing metals).

The conjunction of these specific factors has led to some segments of the component manufacturing industry growing rapidly, as shown in **Exhibit 36**.

Of course, more commoditized parts of the component industry, such as seating, interiors, and gearboxes, are slow-growth components because they typically do not benefit from any of the trends discussed previously. In addition, they suffer from almost no aftermarket demand. In summary, the components that are expected to grow rapidly are the high-value-added components.

[2]Typically, a stop/start system automatically switches off the engine when the car is at a standstill and in neutral and then restarts it as soon as the driver presses the clutch pedal again.

Exhibit 36. Fast-Growth Segments for Component Suppliers

Segment	Growth Rate
Active safety device**	35%
Lane departure warning*	29
Advanced parking assistance*	27
Stop/start systems*	22
Forward collision avoidance*	21
Blind spot detection*	20
Gas direct injection**	17
Common-rail direct fuel injection**	14
Touch screens*	14
Electrification**	12
Electronic stability control*	9
Tire pressure monitoring*	9
Valve train**	5

Notes: *Growth segments based on projected global industry CAGR revenue growth from 2012 until 2020 (Continental, "Fact Book 2013"). **Growth segments based on projected global industry CAGR revenue growth until 2020 (Delphi, "J.P. Morgan Auto Conference," 13 August 2014).

TIRE MANUFACTURERS

INDUSTRY OVERVIEW

The manufacture of tires, although tires are a key component in a car, is usually considered separately from general automotive component manufacturing because of the tire industry's special characteristics.

The first myth that investors need to dispel is that a tire is a simple and homogeneous product that nearly any manufacturer is capable of producing. In fact, it is a complex product with high value-added content. The competitive barriers to entry in the business are high because of (1) high capital intensity (capital expenditures, or capex, are usually at least 6% of sales and can reach 9% if capacity is being expanded), which requires scale to be profitable, and (2) the importance of brands. In addition, tire manufacturing is perhaps the only part of the automotive industry with any pricing power.

The tire industry is also more consolidated, especially in regard to premium tires, than the general automotive component manufacturing industry. Considerable research and development goes into tire manufacturing; R&D is typically 2%–3% of tire sales. Also, years of research go into producing new products designed for existing and expected means of transport. The continuing development of the "green" (eco-friendly) tire is a case in point.[3]

The process of homologation of tire brands, which involves testing and certification of tires by government agencies for conformity to technical standards and issuance of a product rating, is already under way in the European Union. It will further separate the premium, high-value tire segment from the budget tire segments.

Tires have the following critical characteristics that consumers are prepared to pay more for:

- their role in fuel economy and
- safety, as a result of their adherence to the road, wet grip, rolling resistance, and braking distance.

For example, an expensive tire might actually turn out to save the driver more money over the long term than the increased price because its superior quality reduces fuel consumption. Fuel, a particularly significant cost component in owning a truck, can account for 30% of the cost of ownership. Moreover, tires are the second-largest cause of road accidents in trucks. These characteristics are a few of the reasons why tires have some degree of pricing power and why EBIT margins and return on invested capital (ROIC) for tire companies are among the highest in the automotive industry.

[3]For more information, see, for example, RightTurn: www.rightturn.com/green-tires.

Exhibit 37 shows that the global tire industry for passenger cars and trucks has annual revenues of around USD200 billion. This amount is based on 1,460 million light vehicle tires sold worldwide at an average selling price (to dealers) of USD110 per tire and 138 million truck tires sold at an average price of USD300. The tire industry is thus considerably smaller in revenues than either the general automotive component industry or the car manufacturing industry.

Exhibit 37. Size of the Global Tire Market by 2014 Revenues

2014 Revenues	Passenger Car and Light Truck	Heavy Truck
OE units (millions)	420	27
Replacement units	1,040	111
Total units	1,460	138
Average price (USD)	110	300
Total market (USD billions)	161	41

Sources: Continental, "Fact Book 2013"; Michelin, "2013 Annual Report"; author's estimates for 2014.

Global tire demand is expected to increase by more than 5% annually in volume terms until the end of 2020. It is expected to consist of original equipment demand growing by 4% (in line with global car production) and replacement demand growing faster, by 6%. The 6% figure is based on growth in global light vehicles in use of 4% plus increased miles driven in developing markets, which implies an increase in the frequency of tire changes. Currently, car drivers in developing markets drive fewer miles than those in the developed markets.

The high proportion of replacement demand confers a less cyclical profile on tires than the rest of the auto industry and defensive characteristics as an investment, as shown in **Exhibit 38**. Even in a deep recession, such as in 2008 and 2009, tire demand did not fall nearly as fast as car demand or car component demand. Replacement demand is more stable because worn tires simply need to be replaced. A driver of a car with bald tires cannot defer replacement indefinitely. In many countries, legislation requires that they be replaced. In this regard, the tire business is seen by many investors as a more defensive way of investing in the automotive industry.

Exhibit 39 shows the world's top 11 tire manufacturers by 2014 revenues. Compared with the general automotive component manufacturing industry, tire manufacturing is more consolidated; the top five players account for about 44% of industry revenues. Furthermore, these five are the only genuinely global players in the tire industry.

Exhibit 38. Percentage Change in Tire Volumes and Light Vehicle Sales, US Market, 1998–2013

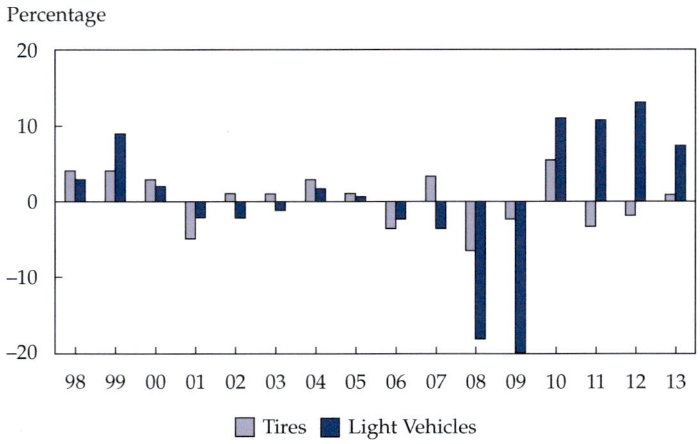

Sources: Cooper Tires (tire data); Bureau of Economic Analysis (light vehicle sales).

Exhibit 39. Top 11 Tire Manufacturers by 2014 Revenues

Manufacturer	Revenue (USD billions)
Bridgestone	29.3
Michelin	24.4
Goodyear	17.8
Continental	12.9
Pirelli	8.0
Sumitomo	6.9
Hankook	6.4
Yokohama	4.8
Cheng Shin	4.3
Cooper	3.5
Kumho	3.3

Source: Statista, "The World's Largest Tire Producers in FY 2014, Based on Tire-Related Sales" (www.statista.com/statistics/225677/revenue-of-the-leading-tire-producers-worldwide).

Exhibit 40 shows the volume market share of the main players in the global tire industry. The top five players account for 48% of industry volume, which is not highly concentrated overall, but the tire manufacturing industry is more consolidated than either the general automotive component industry or the car manufacturing industry.

Exhibit 40. 2013 Volume Market Share of Tire Manufacturers

Manufacturer	Share
Bridgestone	14.6%
Michelin	13.7
Goodyear	9.4
Continental	6.0
Pirelli	4.3
Sumitomo	3.7
Hankook	3.7
Yokohama	2.6
Cheng Shin	2.6
Zhongce Rubber	2.4
GITI	2.0
Cooper	1.8
Kumho	1.8
Toyo	1.6
Others	29.8

Note: Global market share by volume.
Source: Bridgestone, "Bridgestone Data 2015" (www.bridgestone.com/corporate/library/data_book/pdf/BSDATA2015.pdf).

Interestingly, **Exhibit 41** shows that the major players have suffered a significant loss of market share since 2004. The share of the top three manufacturers dropped from 55% in 2003 to less than 38% in 2013. The cause is cheap tire imports from developing nations—China, in particular—and the growth of the budget tire segment in general, from which the global majors are absent.

TIRE MANUFACTURING COMPETITIVE LANDSCAPE

The tire industry owes its high profitability (EBIT margins in the mid- to high teens as a percentage) partly to replacement demand, which accounts for about 70% of tires sold. Distribution channels for replacement tires are fragmented, and tires are

Exhibit 41. Chronic Market Share Loss of Global Major Tire Manufacturers, 1997–2013

Year	Bridgestone	Michelin	Goodyear	Others
1997	18.6%	18.3%	17.1%	46.0%
1998	18.8	19.2	16.8	45.2
1999	19.4	19.4	16.6	44.6
2000	19.7	18.9	19.2	42.2
2001	18.1	19.6	18.2	44.1
2002	18.8	20.1	17.2	43.9
2003	18.3	19.9	16.8	45.0
2004	18.0	19.2	17.7	45.1
2005	17.9	17.5	17.1	47.5
2006	17.2	17.2	16.0	49.6
2007	16.9	17.1	14.9	51.1
2008	16.7	16.3	13.2	53.8
2009	16.2	15.5	12.4	55.9
2010	16.1	14.8	11.2	57.9
2011	15.2	14.6	10.9	59.3
2012	15.3	14.0	10.1	60.6
2013	14.6	13.7	9.4	62.3

Note: Global market share measured by volume.
Source: Bridgestone, "Bridgestone Data 2015" (www.bridgestone.com/corporate/library/data_book/pdf/BSDATA2015.pdf).

often sold to small, independently owned garages and repair shops that have little to no bargaining power with the global majors of the tire industry.

Furthermore, the typical car driver changes tires only every few years and is relatively insensitive to their cost, even if price comparisons are possible with other brands prior to the replacement purchase. Consumer inertia is widespread in the replacement tire market, which enables tire companies to pass through increases in rubber prices relatively easily. In addition, the industry, certainly the global majors, has a track record of stable oligopolistic behavior.

OE tire sales, approximately 30% of total tire sales by volume, operate under different competitive dynamics from those of the replacement market. Although not disclosed, EBIT margins are low for OE suppliers of tires, usually in low single digits or close to zero, because the tire companies are up against demanding car manufacturers that want to produce their cars at the lowest possible prices. Accordingly, tire manufacturers make almost all of their earnings from the replacement market and the better pricing power there. **Exhibit 42** illustrates this point. An EBIT margin of 13.5% overall is typical for a global tire company; it would be composed of a 3% original equipment EBIT margin and an 18% EBIT margin in replacement tires.

Investors are sometimes concerned about rising rubber prices and the impact they have on tire companies' margins. Rubber, both natural and synthetic (butadiene), is a key raw material component of a tire, as shown in **Exhibit 43**. It generally accounts for approximately 50% of cost of goods sold (COGS).

Raw materials, in turn, account overall for about 50% of COGS, as shown in **Exhibit 44**.

Exhibit 42. Split of Replacement and OE Demand

Measure	Replacement	Original Equipment
Volume	70%	30%
Revenue	75	25
EBIT	93	7

Note: Figures shown are shares summing to 100% for each measure.

Exhibit 43. Breakdown of Raw Materials in Michelin's 2014 Registration Document

Raw Material	Percentage
Natural rubber	28
Synthetic rubber	25
Fillers	19
Chemicals	13
Steel cord	9
Textile	6

Source: Michelin, "2014 Registration Document" (3 March 2015).

Exhibit 44. Breakdown of COGS for a Tire Manufacturer

Input Costs	Percentage of COGS
Raw materials	50–55
Labor	20–30
Other	15–30

Source: Cooper Tire, investor presentation (March 2013).

Investor fears about rising rubber prices are largely unjustified, however, because in the replacement market, tire companies typically succeed in passing on rubber price increases. All or nearly all of the competitors follow. Also, price increases are generally accepted by consumers.

In OE markets, automotive manufacturers have raw material pass-through clauses written into contracts with tire companies. These clauses oblige the tire companies to pass on changes in rubber prices, so there is a limited impact on the tire companies from changes in the price. Accordingly, they do not have the same ability to take advantage of changes in the rubber price to boost their margins.

In fact, rising rubber prices are a good excuse for the tire companies to increase prices, so the impact is often favorable for their margins. They react promptly to changes in the rubber price. Margins can also benefit from a decline in rubber prices, as they have been doing since early 2011 (see **Exhibit 45** and **Exhibit 46**).

Exhibit 45. Sustained Fall in Natural Rubber Prices, 2004–2014

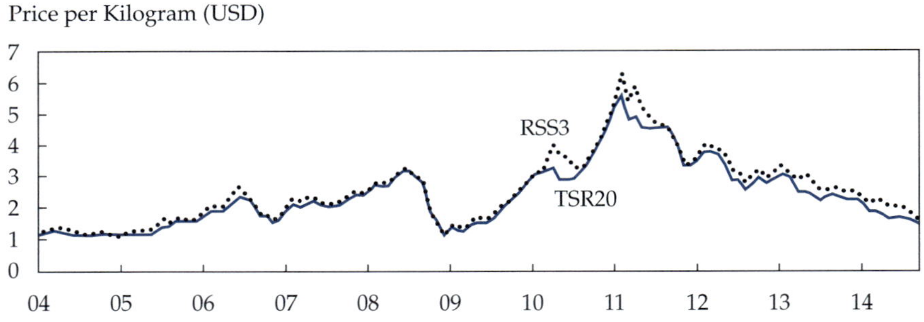

Notes: TSR20 is a technically specified rubber contract, traded in sizes of five metric tons. RSS3 is a type of sheet rubber (ribbed smoked sheet rubber).
Source: Michelin Q3 2014 sales report.

Exhibit 46. Sustained Fall in Synthetic Rubber Prices, 2004–2014

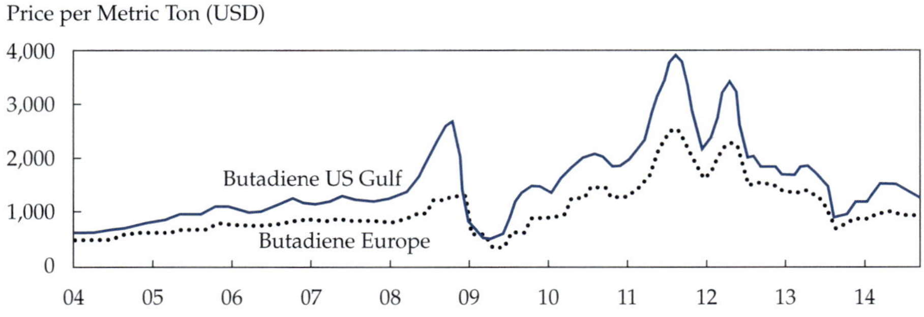

Source: Michelin Q3 2014 sales report.

Tire manufacturers tend to pass falling rubber prices on to the consumer slowly. This timing advantage provides better margins when rubber prices are falling. So, the trend in rubber prices is almost immaterial to tire manufacturers' margins, although, of course, falling rubber prices makes increasing margins easier.

PREMIUM TIRES

The premium tire segment displays all the positive characteristics of the tire manufacturing industry—good margins, pricing power, and consolidated structure—to an even greater degree.

The definition of a premium tire is varied. Traditionally, it is any tire more than 17 inches in diameter. Pirelli defines it as a "high performance" tire, which is more constrained than peer definitions because it refers to speed codes rather than tire size. Winter tires are also considered premium, which is certainly true from a profitability perspective.

Typically, the characteristics of a premium tire are as follows:

- It is more complex to manufacture.
- It costs about double the price of a standard tire.
- It is significantly more profitable than a standard tire (three times as profitable as a standard tire, according to Pirelli).
- Growth in the segment is three times that of standard tires.

Pricing power is also greater in premium tires because they are usually fitted to premium autos, which are owned by high-income consumers with little price sensitivity. In addition, owners of premium cars typically drive them twice the distance of other cars, so more frequent tire changes are required.

The premium tire industry is more insulated from cheap imports from developing countries than is the standard tire segment and is also, with only five major players, more consolidated. The five are Continental, Nokian, Bridgestone, Michelin, and Pirelli. This consolidation leads to the pricing power. In contrast, consumers of standard tires have a choice of about 30 companies from which to purchase tires.

Premium tires account for 23% of total global tire sales by volume, and the premium segment is leading in growth, as highlighted in **Exhibit 47**.

Profit margins are significantly higher in premium tires, as highlighted in **Exhibit 48**, which shows that for Pirelli, the larger the tire, the higher the EBIT margin earned.

Michelin does not break out premium tires from standard tires. A significant part (39% of volume) of its car and light truck segment is premium, but it also has a high-margin specialty tires division that is essentially the supersized industrial type of tire

Exhibit 47. Volume Growth Rates of Premium and Standard Tires Worldwide

	Tire Type		
	Standard	Premium	Global Market Size (million units)
2012	79%	21%	1,327
2013e	78	22	1,359
2014e	77	23	1,410
2015e	76	24	1,466
2016e	75	25	1,515
2017e	74	26	1,564

Notes: 2013–17 CAGR: standard = 2.4%; premium = 7.3%; total market = 3.6%. e = estimate.
Source: Pirelli, "2013–2017 Industrial Plan" (6 November 2013): http://pid2013.iwebcasting.it/assets/files/booklet.pdf.

Exhibit 48. Pirelli's 2013 Light Vehicle Tire EBIT Margin by Tire Size

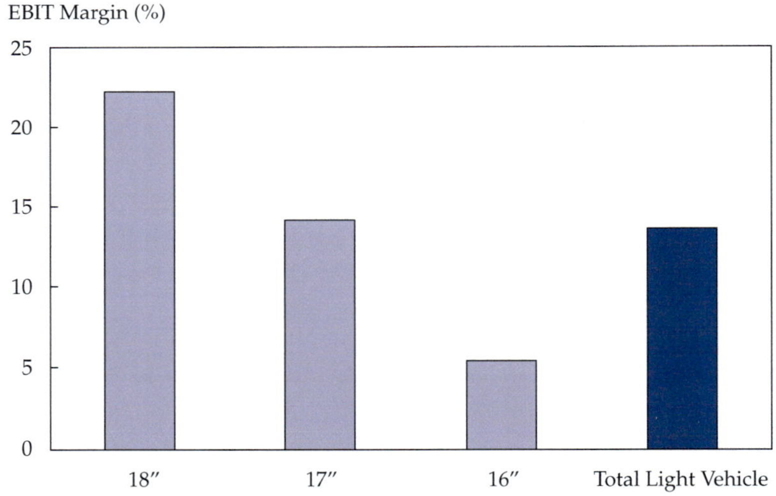

Note: Total light vehicle EBIT margin is before restructuring charges.
Source: Pirelli, "2013–2017 Industrial Plan" (6 November 2013): http://pid2013.iwebcasting.it/assets/files/booklet.pdf.

that construction, agricultural, and mining vehicles or aircraft might use. They are several times the size and cost of a truck or passenger car tire and are very premium.

Michelin and Bridgestone essentially represent a global duopoly in the specialty tire market. This market dominance explains Michelin's high EBIT margin (shown in **Exhibit 49**), which was down significantly in both 2013 and 2014 from its 2012 level of 26.0%. The cause was severe weakness in infrastructural equipment and the onset of weakness and inventory drawdown in the mining equipment sector at the end of 2013.

Winter tires are also considered premium tires and have the profitability profile to match. Nokian, the Finland-based manufacturer and producer of winter tires, reported passenger car tire EBIT margins of 33%–34% for 2011–2013, as shown in **Exhibit 50**.

Nokian's 2014 EBIT margin in passenger car tires fell to just above 29% following the collapse of the Russian market and the considerable depreciation of the Russian ruble. Even so, this margin is high for a tire company. Nokian is unique, however, because it has high market shares in its key geographical regions (Scandinavia, Russia, central Europe) and uses low-cost Russia as a production hub for supplying tires to both Russia and Europe. Also, it supplies only the profitable replacement market, not the original equipment market, where margins are usually negligible. Other tire companies are unlikely to be able to boast these types of margins in their winter tire business.

Exhibit 49. Michelin's 2014 EBIT Margin by Segment

Segment	EBIT Margin
Car and light truck	10.5%
Truck	8.1
Specialty	19.3
Total company	11.1

Source: Presentation of Michelin 2014 results, company website.

Exhibit 50. Nokian's Winter Tire Business, 2011–2014

Year	EBIT Margin
2011	34.1%
2012	33.7
2013	33.3
2014	29.1

Note: Passenger car division.
Source: Nokian company reports.

FUEL ECONOMY AND EMISSIONS CONTROL

Environmental concerns are well documented in the automotive market. Governments and regulatory bodies across the world are attempting to control greenhouse gas emissions. In the European Union, road transport contributes 20% of all CO_2 emissions, with 12% coming directly from passenger cars. In the United States, transportation contributes 28% of all CO_2 emissions. Although cars have become more fuel efficient and "cleaner" over many years, the number of cars in use has significantly increased, offsetting the reduction in emissions per vehicle.

Emissions standards include legal requirements governing air pollution that have set quantitative limits. No single emissions standard applies around the world. Instead, each national government and the EU have set their own standards for vehicle emissions. They are usually expressed in terms of energy intensity, such as miles per gallon (mpg, US terminology), liters per 100 kilometers driven (l/100km, European terminology), or grams of CO_2 emission per kilometer driven (g/km).

Exhibit 51 highlights the progress made in reducing passenger vehicle emissions and the stringent targets that governments hope to introduce for 2020 and beyond. In the EU, one of the first regions in the world to legislate mandatory limits

Exhibit 51. Emissions Standards: Actual and Targets

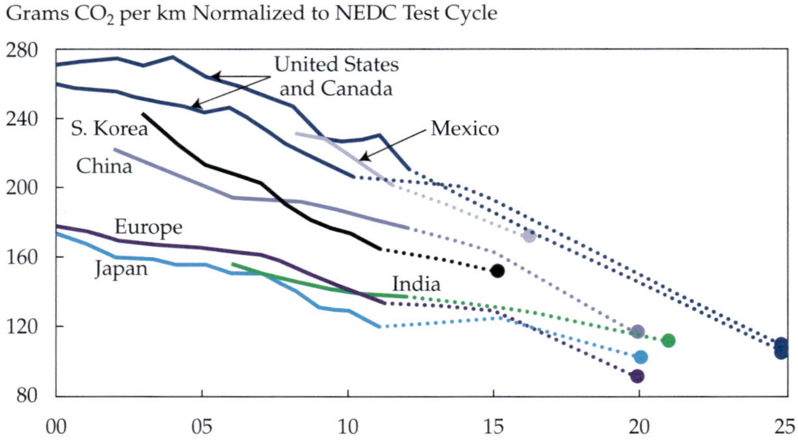

Note: Solid line shows historical performance; dotted line shows target.
Source: Delphi and National Highway Traffic Safety Administration (NHTSA), February 2014.

on emissions, emissions standards for 2015 (130 g/km) were attained in 2013, two years ahead of target.

In the EU, emissions targets are applied to car manufacturers on the basis of the weight of the cars they produce. The reasoning is that heavier cars consume more fuel as a starting point because of the increased weight to be displaced while being driven. So, as shown in **Exhibit 52**, makers of relatively small, light cars—such as Peugeot and Fiat—naturally have lower emissions targets than Daimler, whose car production is more for the executive car and luxury sedan market.

A diesel engine is more fuel efficient than a gasoline-powered engine, and diesel has widespread adoption in Europe and India. In North America, Japan, and China, however, gasoline is the predominant fuel.

Exhibit 52. EU Emissions Standards per Manufacturer (Liters per 100 kilometer [grams CO_2 per kilometer])

	Status 2012	Target 2020
EU average	5.3 (132)	3.8 (95)
Fiat	4.7 (118)	3.4 (86)
PSA (Peugeot Citroën)	4.9 (122)	3.8 (94)
Toyota	4.9 (122)	3.7 (93)
Renault–Nissan	5.1 (128)	3.7 (93)
Ford	5.2 (129)	3.7 (92)
Volkswagen	5.3 (133)	3.8 (96)
GM (Opel)	5.4 (134)	3.9 (97)
BMW	5.5 (138)	4.0 (100)
Daimler	5.7 (143)	4.0 (101)

Notes: 2015 and 2020 targets were calculated under the assumption of no future change to 2012 vehicle weight (European Environmental Agency, 2013). Vehicle weight is "mass in running order"—that is, the weight of an empty vehicle +75 kilograms.

Source: International Council on Clean Transportation, *European Vehicle Market Statistics Pocketbook* (2013).

Car manufacturers have adopted a number of strategies to comply with emissions regulations and to improve the fuel efficiency of their vehicles. They are developing alternative power trains, such as electric vehicles (discussed in the next section of this report), hybrid vehicles, plug-in hybrids, and compressed natural gas vehicles. To date, these alternative fuel technologies have met with limited success. As **Exhibit 53** shows, they account for only around 1% of all cars manufactured. The traditional internal combustion engine (ICE) remains the most significant power train in new cars.

Exhibit 53. Penetration of Alternative Fuel Technologies

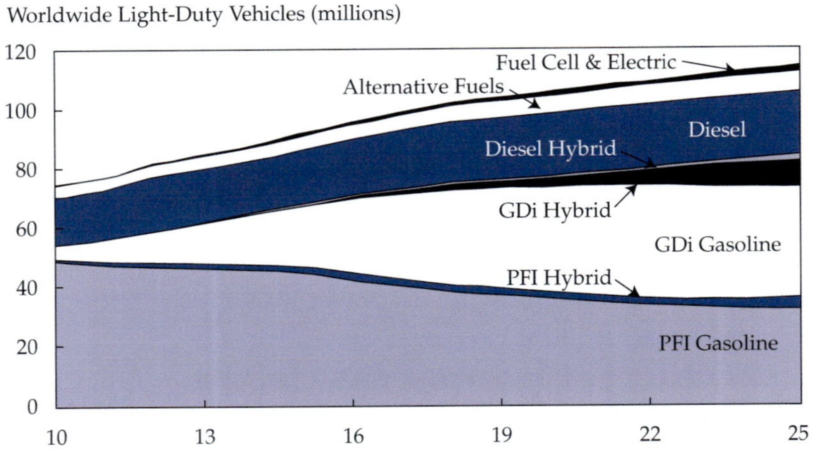

Note: PFI is port fuel injection; GDI is gasoline direct injection.
Source: Delphi, investor presentation (2014).

Measures taken for the mainstream power trains (diesel and gasoline cars) include the following:

- downsizing engines (same output from lower displacement);
- boosting engine power via the use of turbochargers;
- making lighter vehicles (because they consume less fuel), with increased use of aluminum and plastics;
- increasing the number of gears; and
- introducing direct fuel injection, stop/start technology, and dual clutch transmissions.

Some of these alternative fuel technologies currently represent a relatively expensive way of improving fuel economy, as **Exhibit 54** demonstrates.

Increased environmental concerns and emissions standards are contributing to increasing material and component content per car. Estimates range from USD1,000 to USD2,000 per car to meet emissions standards by 2020. Taking the midpoint of USD1,500 and multiplying it by unit sales worldwide of more than 115 million cars by 2020, the global industry bill for complying with emissions standards could be estimated at more than USD170 billion. The incremental cost increases of each gram of CO_2 reduction are shown in **Exhibit 55**.

Exhibit 54. Cost of Incremental Improvement in Fuel Efficiency by Technology

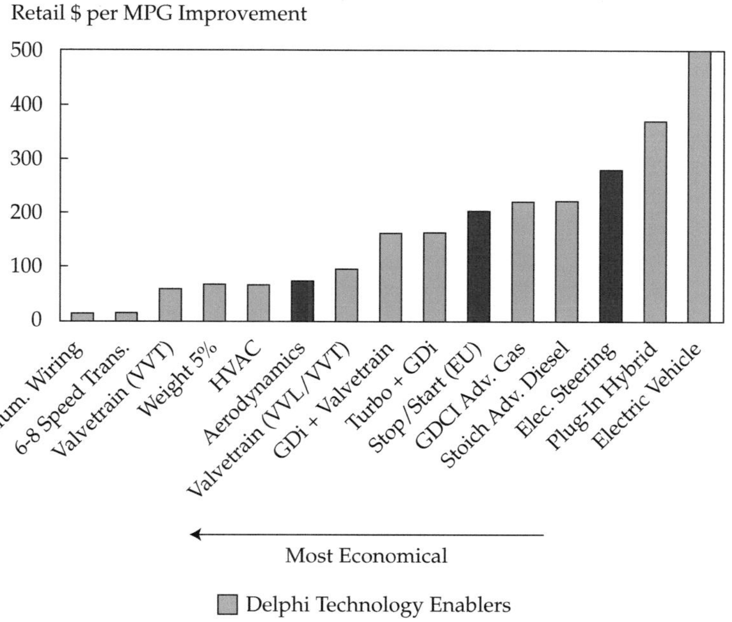

Source: Delphi and NHTSA (February 2014).

Improvements in fuel efficiency brought about by emissions standards legislation are a key argument in selling a car, so the manufacturers of the most fuel-efficient cars will be best placed to command some pricing power and pass on at least part of those costs to the consumer. Fuel efficiency is a key criterion that consumers are willing to pay for because it procures them a financial benefit. Long term, to remain competitive, car manufacturers will need to invest in R&D to innovate and conceive new products with their suppliers to improve fuel efficiency.

The quest for improved fuel economy is increasing the cost base of car manufacturers but, at the same time, providing increased business for the component suppliers. The realization that this cost headwind for car manufacturers is a revenue tailwind for car component manufacturers causes some investors to first seek investment opportunities among the component suppliers.

Exhibit 55. Incremental Cost of CO_2 Emissions Control

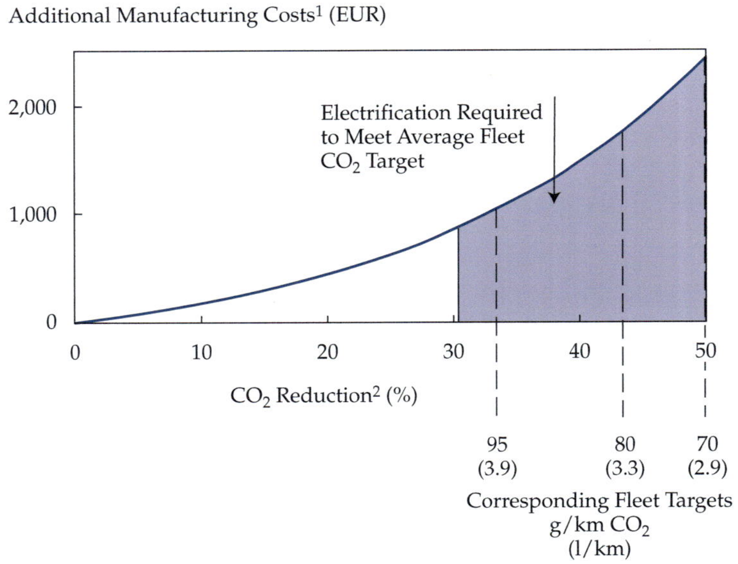

[1]Anticipated for 2020; average for gasoline and diesel ICEs.
[2]Relative to 2010 baseline.
Source: International Council on Clean Transportation and McKinsey & Company report: www.mckinsey.com.

PROSPECTS FOR THE ELECTRIC CAR

INDUSTRY OVERVIEW

Given the preceding section on fuel economy, the concept of an electric car might appear to be a dream come true for legislators, car manufacturers, and consumers alike—but it is not so simple.

The electric car has existed in different forms since the early 20th century. Its earlier use was quickly superseded by the mass production of cars with low-cost combustion engines from the 1920s on. The modern version of the electric car is in its infancy.

There are three types of electric car:

1. Battery electric vehicle (BEV). This car is based on an entirely electric drive train powered by an electric battery without the support of an ICE. This vehicle, therefore, does not require any gasoline. The electric battery needs to be charged, although it can benefit from some recharging through the braking process, whereby some of the energy is recovered that is normally converted to heat by braking. Typically, BEVs are most suited to small passenger cars.

2. Plug-in hybrid electric vehicle (PHEV). This vehicle runs on an electric drive train powered by an electric battery, but it also has the support of an ICE that can take over propulsion from the electric battery and can also recharge the battery. All of the energy in a PHEV comes from the electricity grid. It depletes the electric battery before it uses the ICE.

3. Hybrid electric vehicle (HEV). An HEV has two complementary drive systems—(1) a gasoline engine and fuel tank and (2) an electric motor, battery, and controls. These systems operate together to propel the car. Typically known simply as "hybrids," HEVs are not considered electric cars by some experts because all of the energy comes from the gasoline engine and what is known as "regenerative braking"—by which the electric motor that normally drives the vehicle is essentially operated in reverse (electrically) during braking or coasting. Also, the vehicle cannot be charged from the electricity grid.

HEVs have been in existence since the 1990s and account for the bulk of the electric car market. Development took off with the launch in 1997 of the Toyota Prius. HEVs attained a 5% market share of new car sales in 2012 in both North America and Europe, compared with around 20% of Japanese new car sales.

Unlike an HEV, both BEVs and PHEVs plug into the electricity grid. The main difference between the two is that the range of the PHEV is greater than that of the BEV because the PHEV can revert to its ICE.

If we define the electric car market to include only BEVs and PHEVs, then electric vehicles account for a marginal share of automobile sales, less than 1% in the developed world, so the concept is still a niche one. Cumulative global sales of the modern generation of electric cars in the four years to the end of September 2014 reached 600,000 units, of which 260,000 are accounted for by the US market.

Exhibit 56 shows that sales are largely concentrated in the developed world. China is the only country in the developing world with a significant number of electric vehicles.

Exhibit 57 lists the major makes and models of electric or semi-electric vehicles as of November 2014. Although more than 100 electric car models are currently

Exhibit 56. Concentration of Electric Vehicle Sales in Developed Markets, 2012 vs. 2013

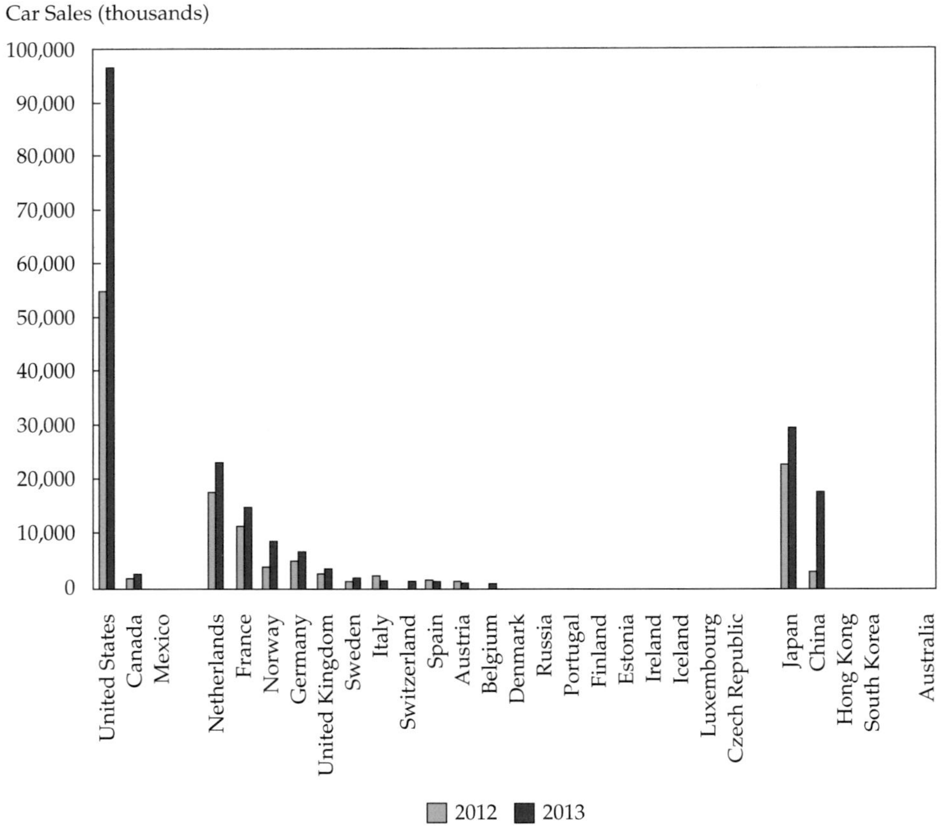

Source: UK Institute of Transport Studies.

available, only about 25 are mass-produced. The market is currently dominated by four models: Nissan Leaf, Chevy Volt, Toyota Prius, and Tesla Model S. Cumulative sales of the Nissan Leaf, launched in December 2010, numbered more than 150,000 units by November 2014. The Chevy Volt (including the Ampera model sold in Europe), which was launched at the same time, reached 87,000 units. The Toyota Prius, a hybrid electric car first launched in Japan in 1997 and introduced worldwide in 2000, had reached cumulative sales of 4.8 million units by September 2014. The Tesla Model S, a full electric vehicle, reached cumulated global sales of 50,000 units by late 2014.

Exhibit 57. Major Electric Vehicle Models, as at November 2014

Electric Vehicles		PHEV	
Make	Model	Make	Model
BMW	i3	Audi	A3 e-tron
Chevrolet	Spark	BMW	i3 REX
Fiat	500e	BMW	i8
Ford	Focus	Cadillac	ELR
Honda	Fit	Chevrolet	Volt
Kia	Soul	Ford	C-Max Energi
Mercedes-Benz	B-class	Ford	Fusion Energi
Mitsubishi	i	Honda	Accord
Nissan	Leaf	McLaren	P1
Smart	Fortwo	Mercedes-Benz	S550
Tesla	Model S (60kWh)	Porsche	918 Spyder
Tesla	Model S (85kWh)	Porsche	Cayenne S
Toyota	RAV4	Porsche	Panamera S
Volkswagen	e-Golf	Toyota	Prius

Source: Alternative Fuels Data Center, US Department of Energy, "Model Year 2015: Alternative Fuel and Advanced Technology Vehicles" (24 November 2014): www.afdc.energy.gov/uploads/publication/MY2015_afv_atv_2_.pdf.

ADVANTAGES AND DISADVANTAGES

Exhibit 58 provides a simple comparison of electric and gasoline cars. The main advantages of the electric car over the standard ICE car are as follows:

- No air pollution. Because electric vehicles do not emit tailpipe pollutants, they are environmentally friendly. Electricity generation is often not the cleanest of industries, however, because most of electric power is generated from fossil fuels.

- No dependence on oil, a finite fuel resource.
- Use of electricity. It is both cheaper and more predictable in terms of price than oil.
- Improved operating performance. Electric vehicles are quieter, run more smoothly (as a result of the gearless or single-gear design), accelerate better and faster (because the torque of an electric motor is based on electric current, not rotational speed), and need less maintenance than a combustion engine.
- They are more energy efficient. Because an electric vehicle consumes no energy while at rest or coasting, the estimate is that approximately 80% of the energy used by an electric car goes into propulsion of the vehicle, as opposed to 15%–20% for an ICE car (because most energy in the ICE car is wasted in the form of heat).

Exhibit 58. Simple Comparison of Electric and Gasoline Cars

Electric	Gasoline
No tailpipe emissions	Greenhouse gases/pollution
Utility company	OPEC dependence
100± mile range	300+ mile range
Hours to recharge	Minutes to refuel
2 cents per mile	12+ cents per mile

Source: www.plugincars.com.

The following shortcomings of electric vehicles explain why they are viewed as a marginal product in the automotive industry:

- Limited range. The electric car has less range, usually up to 300 km on one charge, than an ICE fueled by gasoline, which typically has a range of 800–900 km on a standard 50-liter tank. The problem appears as “range anxiety” for drivers of electric cars—that is, drivers fear that the energy stored in the electric battery will run out before they reach their destinations.
- Recharging. A full recharge can take up to eight hours. Fast-charging technology is being developed that can cut full-charging times to between 30 minutes

and two hours. This amount of time is still far longer than filling up at the fuel pump.

- Lack of charging infrastructure. Batteries can be charged at home, but otherwise, charging infrastructure is limited, especially outside of large cities. Government austerity measures in recent years have exacerbated the problem because much of the investment in charging stations was provided for or funded by local municipalities or the central government.
- High up-front cost of purchase. The reason the electric car costs so much is the high cost of batteries. The electric battery typically costs USD12,000–USD15,000, which is a significant portion of the car's overall cost. No battery manufacturer has yet devised a method of mass-producing batteries inexpensively. In addition, the battery might need replacing several times in the life of the electric car. Consumers have shown willingness to drive electric cars but not to pay a premium for them.
- Weight and volume. Putting an electric battery in a car considerably increases the weight, making it cumbersome. Electric batteries are also voluminous and can consume space that might have provided additional trunk space.
- Limited choice of models. Currently, the consumer has a choice of only 25 mass-produced electric cars (see Exhibit 57). Electric cars are sold in large numbers only in the United States, Europe, Japan, and China.

The electric car's current shortcomings prevent it from achieving mass-market status, but car manufacturers are working with suppliers to find an answer to some of these issues. Clearly, the future of the electric car depends on finding a cost-effective electric battery, decreasing battery charging times, and reducing the weight of the battery. Also needed is the time to put an improved charging infrastructure in place.

Exhibit 59 highlights the trade-off in terms of battery costs and fuel prices.

The major cost of operating an electric car is the cost of the battery over the life cycle of the car, not the cost of the electricity. Usually, the electric battery cost is measured in terms of cost per kilowatt hour (kWh). In recent years, battery costs have fallen, according to numerous reports, from USD800 per kWh in 2009 to around USD500 per kWh in 2014 and USD300 per kWh in 2015, although car manufacturers are unclear about the cost of their battery packs.

Tesla, the electric car manufacturer, is planning a revolutionary approach to mass-producing battery packs in order to decrease their unit cost. With the help of Panasonic, it is planning to build an electric battery giga-factory in Nevada that will cost USD5 billion and employ 6,500 people to attempt to reduce the unit battery cost to USD100 per kWh or less. Tesla hopes to achieve this goal by 2020. If so, the

Exhibit 59. Trade-Off between Fuel Prices and Battery Costs

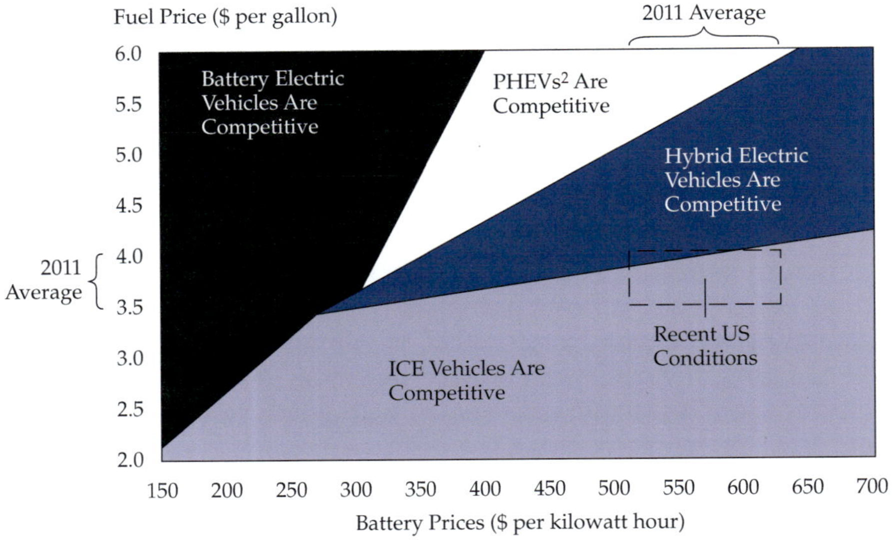

Source: Russell Hensley, John Newman, and Matt Rogers, "Battery Technology Charges Ahead," McKinsey & Company (July 2012): www.mckinsey.com/insights/energy_resources_materials/battery_technology_charges_ahead.

achievement will change the economics of battery production and the cost of the electric car and should significantly boost demand for electric cars.

Reaching the goal, however, might be easier said than done. First, there are the supply constraints on lithium ion, which is needed for rechargeable batteries. It is a rare element so far found only in Latin America, China, and Australia. This situation limits the number of batteries that can be physically and economically produced.

Second, customers are still hesitant as to the electric car and so are car manufacturers. Alternatives to electrification include fuel cell and compressed natural gas technologies, which many manufacturers are also exploring. Some manufacturers are still observing the market and its evolving technologies and waiting for a sufficiently strong signal that the electric vehicle is the technology of the future. To conclude that the electric car is the only way forward is premature. It is likely to be one of several technologies that achieve the same aims of cutting emissions and reducing oil dependency.

Exhibit 60 highlights the Navigant Research projected sales trend of electric cars. Strong sales growth is expected to continue, albeit from a small base. Overall, electric vehicle penetration rates will remain low, unless there is a quantum shift in electric battery technology and cost that makes the proposition economically viable.

Investors can also find opportunities to invest in companies that supply content for electric and hybrid cars, including charging cables, battery components, cell contact systems, pressure exchange systems, and shielding and casing products.

Exhibit 60. Global Sales of Electric Vehicles by Segment, 2012–2020

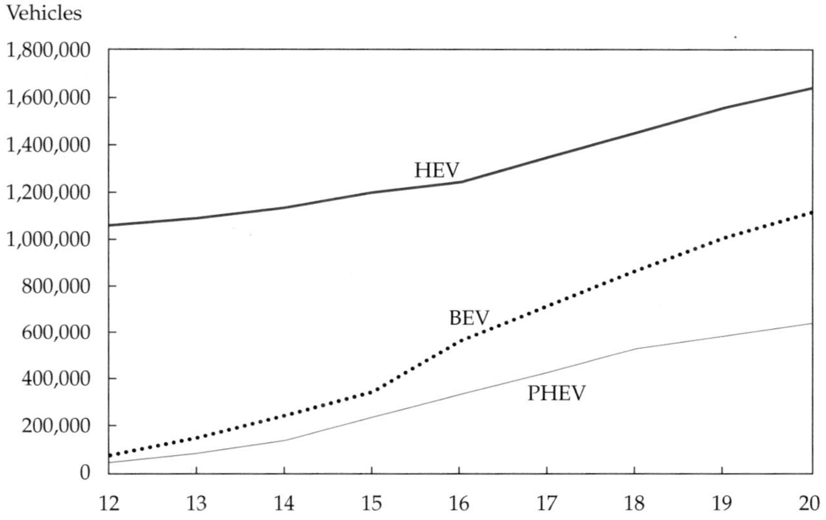

Source: Bradley Berman and John Gartner, "Plug-In Electric Vehicles," Pike Research (Second Quarter 2012): www.navigantresearch.com/wp-content/uploads/2012/06/PEV-12-Executive-Summary.pdf.

RISKS

Aside from the usual operating, financial, and economic risks facing any business, the automotive industry bears specific operating, financial, political and regulatory, and investment risks.

OPERATING RISKS

- The manufacturer's model-launch cycle creates a risk. Investors have no means of knowing whether a car manufacturer's new models will meet with customer approval. If not, significant discounts may be offered to reduce excess inventory. The risk is greater for companies whose model-launch cycles are to be extensive in the forthcoming period. For example, Daimler, the German premium manufacturer, renewed nearly its entire product range during 2013 and 2014.

- Car manufacturers have a history of not communicating price discounting until it has already occurred, by which time the damage to earnings has been done and it is too late for investors to react.

- Judging whether a company is carrying excess inventory and will eventually need to discount prices is difficult because if sales have been slow, the car manufacturer sometimes shifts inventory from its own balance sheet to those of the dealers. As a result, low inventories at the OEM may conceal a worrying underlying trend.

- Logistics pose the potential for supply disruptions. If a parts supplier fails to deliver parts on time, the car cannot be produced and sales are forgone by the manufacturer.

- Industrial action is a possibility. In certain regions, notably Europe and parts of Asia (South Korea), the automotive labor unions are powerful. Strikes can disrupt production.

- High fixed costs in the industry (plant, R&D, depreciation) make earnings volatile. Even small changes in volumes or prices can lead to significant changes in profit, especially for low-margin companies.

The differences in fixed costs by segment are illustrated in **Exhibit 61. Exhibit 62** shows the impact on margins in the segment of a hypothetical new fuel efficiency regulation costing EUR500 per car. Luxury and premium cars can better adapt to a sudden cost shock of this nature because of their higher margins. In the case of the mass-market car, such a new charge wipes out all of the profit margin.

Companies might not be able to pass on the effects of a steep jump in the price of raw materials, such as aluminum or steel. Usually, some protection is built into supplier contracts with OEMs through pass-through clauses, but for replacement parts, the ability to pass on price increases depends on relative pricing power.

Higher oil prices are generally not good news for the automotive industry. They discourage driving, so less tread on tires is worn and fewer tire replacements are needed, and they squeeze consumer budgets, encouraging consumers to delay major purchases and even maintenance. The positive side is that high oil prices encourage drivers to trade in their cars for more energy-efficient ones, and high oil prices shift demand from ICE power trains to hybrid and electric vehicles.

The long-term trend in demand is for smaller cars, including smaller premium cars. The smaller the car, the lower the margin in general. So, the demand trend might be margin dilutive.

Product recall risk has increased because of the advent of platform manufacturing strategies. Although using a common plant platform to manufacture whole ranges of different models improves scale and decreases the unit cost of manufacturing, a recall affects a far greater number of vehicles. Such a recall is more likely than a limited recall to get press attention and to damage the car manufacturer's reputation.

A mild winter can seriously reduce demand for winter tires or delay the start of the season, causing an inventory buildup. Component suppliers have a risk that

Exhibit 61. Hypothetical Cars in Different Segments

Segment	Cost Price (EUR)
Mass	15,000
Premium	40,000
Luxury	80,000

Exhibit 62. Hypothetical Impact on EBIT Margins of EUR500 Cost Shock per Car

Segment	Before	After
Mass	3.0%	–0.3%
Premium	10.0	8.8
Luxury	15.0	14.4

their OEM customers will take production in-house for the component they used to buy. Some component suppliers, especially Asia-based ones, are highly dependent on a parent company or major shareholder for a large portion of their business. This dependence can limit their ability to win new clients and compromise their ability to defend their pricing strategies. Component suppliers are also under constant pressure from OEMs to cut their prices.

Product obsolescence and the inability to innovate to meet market demand can adversely affect earnings for all segments of the automotive industry.

Tire manufacturers are threatened with increased penetration of cheap imports, especially from low-cost developing countries. This risk primarily affects the non-premium segment of the tire market.

FINANCIAL RISKS

In an economic downturn, working capital may suddenly increase if sales slump and a car manufacturer is holding excess inventory. The surge in working capital may lead to a breach of debt covenants and, in serious cases, to inability to pay suppliers, insolvency, or bankruptcy.

Mergers and acquisitions in the automotive manufacturing industry have a poor track record from the point of view of integration and profitability. An overconfident automotive manager might waste shareholder funds by making an unsuccessful acquisition.

Loan loss provisions in car manufacturers' financing divisions can deteriorate suddenly, impairing the company's profitability. These provisions can have a significant impact because finance divisions may generate as much as 20%–25% of a car manufacturer's EBIT.

Changes in the residual value of a car may also have an impact on profitability. Leased cars that are returned need to be written off by the amount of the drop in residual value, which negatively affects the car manufacturer's earnings.

POLITICAL AND REGULATORY RISKS

Government regulation is unlikely to go away. Currently, the most important regulations concern emissions control, fuel economy, and vehicle safety. Regulation, which imposes additional cost burdens on car manufacturers not easily passed on to their final customers, is negative for margins.

The automotive industry attracts the attention of government officials, who consider it an essential industry and strongly object to the threat of potential redundancies (layoffs) or delocalization of a plant. This attention may slow down or even prevent necessary restructuring, causing excess capacity and a suboptimal level of profitability for the industry.

Governments may interfere in market forces. A good example is scrappage schemes that artificially boost demand—usually pulling it from a future period and causing short-lived distortions to sales and earnings of car manufacturers and their suppliers. In such cases, investors have difficulty making the right decisions because they know demand will be sustained for a period but will likely fall off sharply. Then, earnings in some future period will suffer.

Trade barriers are always a threat, especially in difficult economic times. In certain circumstances, governments believe they should demonstrate a preference for domestic production and tax or inhibit imported cars.

INVESTMENT RISKS

Transparency of sales and earnings is notoriously low in the automotive industry, and earnings estimates are frequently revised. The result is shifts in share and bond prices, which lead to changes in valuation multiples.

The industry is highly cyclical, and economic circumstances can change rapidly for the better or the worse, usually without warning. Changes often come faster than a portfolio manager can alter positions to fit a revised investment stance or economic outlook.

Investors have a limited ability to know what is happening in the industry because it is global. Within this worldwide market, pockets of strength may offset pockets of weakness. For example, generalizing the results of surveys undertaken to gauge how a particular model is selling or how pricing is evolving is difficult because the surveys are often local and economic circumstances can change rapidly. Investors need to be wary of taking anecdotal evidence too seriously.

Reliable information is limited on changes in pricing trends, which usually have a more significant bearing on earnings than changes in volume—the metric that investors regularly apply in the automotive industry.

FINANCIAL STATEMENT ANALYSIS

CAR MANUFACTURING

HOW TO ANALYZE THE TOP LINE

In terms of analyzing revenue, isolating the organic growth rate of sales from the published figure is important. The published figure might include changes in the scope of consolidation and currencies, which are factors outside the company's control. In addition, organic growth of sales can be further broken down into volume, price, and mix. Usually, price and mix are combined into one factor, which prevents the investor from having a precise split between the two. Many companies give an indication of the contribution made by mix, however, which allows the investor to deduce the price effects. Sometimes a precise figure is published for pricing, but rarely is the mix's impact quantified because it is difficult to separate from price. Ford Motor amalgamates volume and mix and reports net pricing separately (as shown in **Exhibit 63**).

Price changes are more important than mix or volume as profit determinants. Price changes, unlike volume changes, feed through directly to the bottom line without any offset on the cost side. For a car manufacturer, every 1% change in price requires volumes to move by as much as 3% to generate the same impact on earnings. Pricing is, therefore, a key determinant of earnings.

Investors must check whether pricing could be under pressure—for example, if net pricing is negative—and check that inventories are not accumulating. Inventories are often expressed in number of days' sales, and a typical car manufacturer should have 50–60 days' sales. Anything significantly above this number could be a warning sign that the car manufacturer will be discounting prices to move inventory, especially if a plant has low capacity utilization. The change and direction of change in inventory are more important, however, than its level.

Reliable data on pricing are hard to obtain because the data depend on surveys taken at dealerships, which often give a partial picture. Additionally, pricing is very dependent on particular models and time frames. For example, pricing might be weak then suddenly recover as consumers become aware of a particular model's advantages. Price is a data point at a single instant in time, after which pricing can recover or deteriorate. Thus, the indicator that is relatively difficult to get reliable indications about—is less

Exhibit 63. Ford Automotive Division's 2014 Pretax Profit Comparison with 2013

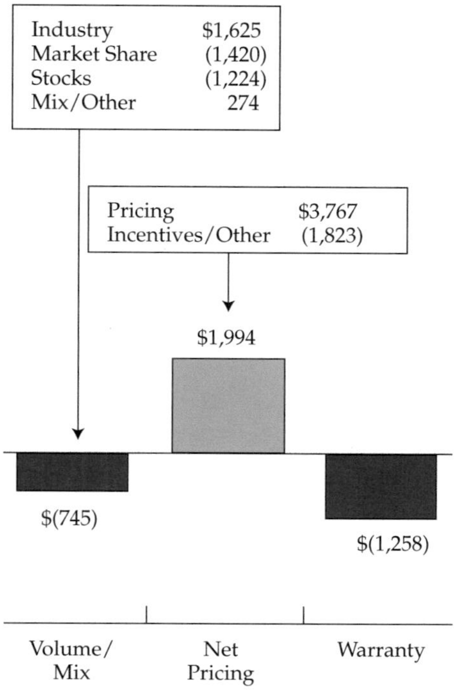

Note: Data in US$ millions; year-on-year change.
Source: Ford Motor Company, "2014 Fourth Quarter and Full Year Earnings Review and 2015 Outlook" (29 January 2015): http://corporate.ford.com/content/dam/corporate/en/investors/investor-events/Quarterly%20Earnings/2014/2014-fourth-quarter-and-full-year-earnings-review-and-2015-outlook-20150128.pdf.

predictable and is more volatile than other factors—has the greatest effect on earnings. This complication is what makes earnings forecasts so inherently difficult for OEMs.

When breaking down revenues, analysts should also take care to review each business's organic growth. Many car manufacturers have other business lines, such as motorbikes or a finance and leasing business.

The mix of products shows details about the changes in the portfolio of sales—that is, whether more luxury models were sold than mass-market models, in which case the mix will be positive. Mix can also be influenced by a car company's model-launch cycle, so a premium car manufacturer might suffer a "negative mix" because its most recent launches were toward the bottom end of the model portfolio. Negative mix, in this case, is not truly negative because model launches enable car manufacturers to gain market share from competitors and maintain pricing. Low-end models also contribute toward covering fixed costs of the plant they are produced in, helping build scale and, in many cases, profitability.

Investors tend to focus on volume because reliable monthly data are published worldwide for all the large markets. These data allow tracking of growth rates, changes in volume trends, and most importantly, whether market share is gained or lost. Market share information is most useful if information is given on a regional basis, such as Volkswagen's data in **Exhibit 64**. The reason is that each car region tends to have varying growth rates. Also, model launches are not simultaneously global. They tend to start in one zone and be progressively rolled out elsewhere in the world.

With regard to sales volume specifically, analysts should check whether a company is gaining or losing market share and try to understand why. The reason for market share loss is important to ascertain. A full pipeline of model launches would be expected to lead to market share gain. Conversely, if a car manufacturer is close to a lull in model launches, it might temporarily lose some share to competitors. Sometimes, a loss is caused by exceptional factors—such as logistics, component shortages, or industrial actions preventing the cars from being produced or delivered to dealers. If the cause is customer dissatisfaction with the company's product, however, then the issue is serious.

Exhibit 64. Volkswagen's 2014 Sales Volume Growth, January to December 2014 vs. 2013
(year-on-year growth in deliveries to customers)

Region	Car Market[a]	Volkswagen Group
North America	6.0%	0.0%
Western Europe	4.9	6.5
Central and Eastern Europe	–6.7	1.3
South America	–11.6	–17.0
Asia Pacific	7.6	11.2
Rest of world	2.2	–2.0

[a]Cars plus light commercial vehicles.

Notes: Data exclude Volkswagen Commercial Vehicles, Scania, and MAN. The Saveiro model, previously Volkswagen Commercial Vehicles, is reported in the Volkswagen passenger cars brand retrospectively as of 1 January 2013.

Source: Hans Dieter Pötsch, "Volkswagen Group: Robust, Innovative, Delivering," Volkswagen investor presentation (March 2015): www.volkswagenag.com/content/vwcorp/info_center/en/talks_and_presentations/2015/03/Geneva.bin.html/binarystorageitem/file/2015-03-03+Geneva+Conference+Presentation.pdf.

DISTORTIONS CREATED BY OEMS' FINANCE AND LEASING BUSINESSES

Almost all of the major global car manufacturers own leasing or finance divisions that provide loans to car buyers. At the end of the car lease, the customer can return the car if the customer prefers not to purchase it. The car manufacturer will then compare the residual value of the car with the book value and may be required to write off any excess value, which reduces earnings. Residual values are thus important to the overall earnings of the car manufacturer.

The leasing and finance business tends to create some distortion in consolidated accounts. It often contributes 20%–25% of EBIT, compared with less than 10% contribution to revenues (these divisions are currently extremely profitable, high-margin businesses). In addition, loans to customers are consolidated on the balance sheet, which often leads to high debt levels, even if the automobile business is in a net positive cash position. Therefore, looking at a consolidated cash flow statement or balance sheet without having the leasing and finance division split out is almost meaningless.

BMW's balance sheet (**Exhibit 65**) shows the considerable amount of consolidated assets and liabilities arising from the finance and leasing business. In fact,

Exhibit 65. Summarized Balance Sheet of BMW, 2014 (EUR millions)

Entry	Group	Automotive	Motorcycles	Financial Services	Other Entities	Elimination
Noncurrent assets	97,959	36,425	359	75,699	29,822	–44,346
of leased products	30,165	3	—	35,366	—	–5,204
of receivables, sales financing	37,438	—	—	37,438	—	—
Current assets	56,844	42,706	511	30,617	38,352	–55,342
Total assets	154,803	79,131	870	106,316	68,174	–99,688
Equity	37,437	31,045	0	9,357	12,031	–14,996
Noncurrent provisions and liabilities	58,288	14,317	595	43,801	28,755	–29,180
Current provisions and liabilities	59,078	33,769	275	53,158	27,388	–55,512
Total equity and liabilities	154,803	79,131	870	106,316	68,174	–99,688

Source: BMW Group, "Annual Report 2014" (2014): www.bmwgroup.com/e/0_0_www_bmwgroup_com/investor_relations/finanzberichte/geschaeftsberichte/2014/_pdf/12507_GB_2014_en_Finanzbericht_Online.pdf.

they are greater than those of the automotive division itself. On the asset side, there are substantial amounts (EUR30.2 billion and EUR32.6 billion, respectively) representing leased product and receivables from sales financing. Attempts to calculate net debt from the consolidated balance sheet could lead to an erroneous result of several tens of billions of euros when, in fact, the automotive division of BMW has net cash of EUR12 billion. This net cash is often referred to as "industrial liquidity" or "industrial net cash."

Investors must be careful to separate out these financial businesses and isolate ratios in each of them rather than calculating EBIT margin or return on equity (ROE) for the whole company. Each constituent business has different profitability, asset efficiency, and capital intensity. **Exhibit 66** shows the differences at BMW; differences could be much larger for other companies.

Exhibit 66. Divisional Split of BMW's EBIT Margins and ROE, 2014

Division	ROE	EBIT Margin
Automotive	14.6%	9.6%
Financial services	13.5	8.5
BMW Group	15.9	11.3

Note: ROE is calculated as the ratio of net income to average equity.
Source: BMW Group, "Annual Report 2014" (2014): www.bmwgroup.com/e/0_0_www_bmwgroup_com/investor_relations/finanzberichte/geschaeftsberichte/2014/_pdf/12507_GB_2014_en_Finanzbericht_Online.pdf.

Similarly, the cash flow statement will include major movements of items in working capital related to the finance business—for example, creditors and debtors that have nothing to do with the core automotive division. So, an analyst will find it useful to look at the company's earnings presentation, usually available online, to analyze the cash flow statement for the automotive division alone, or at least how the automotive division affected the business in terms of cash flow or free cash flow generation, as highlighted in **Exhibit 67** for Volkswagen.

Another reason for caution about the leasing and finance businesses is their impact on the geographical split of EBIT. Many car manufacturers provide this geographical split of group EBIT, which includes all the businesses consolidated—for example, automotive, financial services, motorcycles. The numbers in **Exhibit 68** relate to Toyota's last set of annual accounts for the year ending March 2015.

Toyota's financial services business is spread across the world but has high exposure in North America, which could account for 50% of this division's revenues and 75% of EBIT (respectively, JPY830.6 billion and JPY271.4 billion). Subtracting these figures from the North America totals reveals a more accurate picture of Toyota's

Exhibit 67. Volkswagen's Cash Flow Statement for the Automotive Division Only, January–December 2014 (EUR billions)

Measure	2014
Cash flow from operating activities	21.6
Capex	–11.5
Capitalized R&D costs	–4.6
Other	0.4
Net cash flow before equity investments	5.9
Acquisition and disposal of equity investments	0.2
Net cash flow	6.1

Source: Hans Dieter Pötsch, "Volkswagen Group: Robust, Innovative, Delivering," Volkswagen investor presentation (March 2015): www.volkswagenag.com/content/vwcorp/info_center/en/talks_and_presentations/2015/03/Geneva.bin.html/binarystorageitem/file/2015-03-03+Geneva+Conference+Presentation.pdf.

Exhibit 68. Toyota's Geographical Split of Sales and EBIT, Year Ending March 2015

Area	Sales	EBIT	EBIT Margin
Japan	JPY14,403.8	JPY1,571.4	10.9%
North America	9,677.5	584.5	6.0
Europe	2,848.2	81.1	2.8
Asia	4,981.2	421.7	8.5
Other	2,449.2	111.5	4.6
Elimination	–7,125.7	–19.8	—
Group total	JPY27,234.5	JPY2,750.5	10.1%
Financial services	JPY1,661.1	JPY361.8	21.8%

Source: Toyota, "Supplemental Material for Financial Results for FY2015 (Consolidated)": www.toyota-global.com/investors/financial_result/2015/pdf/q4/consolidated.pdf.

North American car manufacturing operations. If the adjustment is done on this basis, North America's EBIT margin is only 3.5%, well below the overall reported North American EBIT margin of 6.0%. The reason is that a highly profitable business unit is consolidated within it, which boosts the zone's profitability. The car division by itself is not particularly profitable within North America.

Investors should note that a car's profit is usually booked where it is manufactured, not where it is sold. So, Toyota's exports from Japan to North America are booked as Japanese profits, not North American profits. Similarly, BMW exporting German-made cars to China is booked under European profits. Any foreign exchange gains or losses from these export activities are also booked in the originating country of export.

SPECIAL TREATMENT OF CHINESE OPERATIONS

The Chinese authorities require foreign car manufacturers wishing to manufacture cars in China to operate under a joint venture agreement with a local company. Typically, the foreign OEM takes a 50% stake in the joint venture. Also, foreign OEMs can have a maximum of only two joint venture partners.

OEMs usually account for their joint venture share of earnings as an equity affiliate. Therefore, the business is not globally consolidated. Until recently, Nissan proportionally consolidated its Chinese operations, which had a favorable effect on margins because China is a high-margin country for most foreign car manufacturers. Nissan recently changed, however, to treating those operations as an equity affiliate.

Investors should note that the joint venture restrictions do not apply to component suppliers or to tire companies, which can legally operate in China independently without a partner. As a result, a company such as Toyota, which operates under the *keiretsu* system (as discussed in the section on component suppliers) will report the results of many different businesses as equity earnings. For example, its Chinese operations and earnings of all the stakes in its automotive component suppliers are reported this way.

Toyota actually provides a split of its equity earnings by geography, breaking it into Japan, China, and other countries, as shown in **Exhibit 69**. In this instance, China

Exhibit 69. Toyota's Geographical Split of Equity Earnings, FY2014 and FY2015 (JPY billions)

	Equity Earnings		
Country	FY2014	FY2015	Change
Japan	201.2	192.8	–4.2%
China	86.3	83.2	–3.6
Other	30.8	32.4	5.2
Total	318.3	308.5	–3.1%

Note: Toyota's fiscal year ends in March.
Source: Toyota Motor Corporation, "FY2015 Financial Results" (8 May 2015): www.toyota-global.com/investors/financial_result/2015/pdf/q4/presentation.pdf.

includes Toyota's Chinese car manufacturing associate earnings and the earnings of its component supplier stakes earned in China.

Accounting for Chinese businesses is more complicated, however, than this simple illustration. Premium German car manufacturers earn profits at two separate levels on their businesses in China:

- the equity affiliate contribution from the manufacturing operations in China and
- the profit from cars exported from Germany and on car components exported to their own businesses and also sold to competitors, both of which activities are fully consolidated.

Because of the full consolidation of the parts businesses, part of the Chinese business appears in a car manufacturer's consolidated accounts while the profit contribution appears at the equity associate level. Because China is usually highly profitable, this provides a boost to margins. Car manufacturers whose exposure to China is large or that import a relatively high percentage of their local sales into China from abroad obtain the largest benefit.

PROFIT MARGINS

Investors tend to concentrate on EBIT margins and attach less importance to other margins, such as gross margin. Differences between International Financial Reporting Standards (IFRS) and US GAAP accounting can cause significant distortions of gross margins when a comparison of companies reporting under the different systems is made. The reason is that US GAAP includes many operating costs within COGS, which depresses gross margin relative to IFRS reporting.

Distortions still occur at the EBIT level between companies reporting under the same accounting method because individual practices on reporting can differ between companies—for example, companies using different depreciation lives. Nevertheless, EBIT is one of the preferred margins investors analyze.

A useful approach is to check what is known as the EBIT "bridge," the variance in EBIT often contained in an investor results presentation. The bridge shows which factors influenced the change in EBIT from one period to another. It is shown for Toyota for the year ending March 2015 in **Exhibit 70**.

The increase in Toyota's EBIT (+20%) and EBIT margin (from 8.9% to 10.1%) in the year to March 2015 looks impressive. The EBIT bridge, however, allows us to see that it is mostly a result of exchange rate movements caused by a significantly weaker yen translating into a large earnings benefit and the result of cost cutting—factors that may turn out to be transient and unsustainable in future periods.

What is required in an EBIT bridge is detail on the contribution to changes in EBIT made by pricing, mix, and volumes, as is shown for Nissan in **Exhibit 71**.

Nissan's EBIT increase in the year to March 2015 also shows that a large amount of the increase is the result of currencies and significant purchasing cost reductions, although there is a benefit from rising volumes/mix too.

Exhibit 70. Toyota's EBIT Bridge, Year Ending March 2015

Entry	JPY (billions)
Operating income, April 2013–March 2014	2,292.1
Effects of foreign exchange rates	280
Cost reduction efforts	280
Marketing efforts	–70
Increase in expenses, etc.	–160
Valuation gains/losses from interest rate swaps	61.9
Other	66.5
Operating income, April 2014–March 2015	2,750.5

Source: Toyota Motor Corporation, "FY2015 Financial Results" (8 May 2015): www.toyota-global.com/investors/financial_result/2015/pdf/q4/presentation.pdf.

Exhibit 71. Nissan's EBIT Bridge, Year Ending March 2015

Entry	JPY (billions)
Operating income, April 2013–March 2014	498.4
Foreign exchange	68.6
Purchase cost reduction (including raw material)	112.7
Volume/mix	32.4
Marketing/selling expenses	–43.8
US remarketing	–39.5
R&D expenses	–0.1
Manufacturing expenses	–20.1
Other items	–19.0
Operating income, April 2014–March 2015	589.6

Note: Based on accounting for the Chinese manufacturing joint ventures as equity associates.
Source: Nissan Motor Corporation, "Fiscal Year 2014 Financial Results" (13 May 2015): www.nissan-global.com/EN/DOCUMENT/PDF/FINANCIAL/PRESEN/2014/2014results_presentation_968_e.pdf.

OTHER ITEMS—INVENTORY, R&D, CAPEX, MODEL CYCLE, PENSION DEFICITS

Care needs to be taken when looking at inventories of new cars produced. Car manufacturers can move these items off their balance sheets and pass them on to the dealers' balance sheets. This practice may give a misguided view that inventory is under control when, in fact, a considerable number of unsold cars may remain in inventory, which the car manufacturer might need to discount to reduce that inventory.

Another useful check is how much a car manufacturer is spending on R&D and capex. Total R&D, whether capitalized or not, is the correct figure to take into consideration. Typically, the manufacturer should spend 5% of automotive revenues on each, for 10% in total.

A car manufacturer's model cycle is important to investors, but it can be a poor determinant of a company's performance if a new model is not well received by consumers. Some investors believe in what is known as "model-cycle investing"—that investors should buy a stock prior to a period of extensive model launches and revamps. The assumption is that model cycles are "lumpy," with bulges in product launches, but in reality, most car manufacturers attempt to avoid a clustering of new launches. They prefer to spread them out over an extended and evenly spaced period of time. This preference makes sense because model revamps involve additional costs in terms of R&D, labor, material, and marketing.

Model launches do help boost sales because of the refreshing effect they have on the manufacturer's product offerings. Also, they enable the manufacturer to hold the line on pricing. An aging product portfolio is likely to be more susceptible to price discounting because consumers do not want to buy an old car model when the competition is launching plenty of novelties. In addition, if a consumer knows a particular model will change soon, he or she may wait for the new model.

Model-cycle investing requires precise timing, which is not obvious. Invest too early and you run the risk of higher-than-anticipated launch costs and not enough revenue or profit from the proposed launches. Invest too close to the launch and you run the risk that the market has already discounted the event, resulting in a missed opportunity.

Pension deficits need to be taken into account in the calculation of enterprise value (i.e., market capitalization *plus market value of net debt, plus market value of minority interests, minus market value of associates and major stakes, plus net pension liability/minus net pension surplus).* Pension liabilities may be off balance sheet and very long term in nature, but the car manufacturer is obligated to pay them when the time comes, so pension obligations are a debt. This amount should be netted against industrial liquidity or added to industrial net debt to get an inclusive picture of the car manufacturer's indebtedness.

COMPONENT SUPPLIERS AND TIRE MANUFACTURERS

Fortunately, the financial statements of component suppliers and tire manufacturers are not fraught with such a level of complexity as are those of car manufacturers. Component suppliers and tire manufacturers have no finance or leasing divisions, and they usually fully consolidate their Chinese operations because China's authorities do not require a foreign supplier to partner with a local manufacturer.

Organic growth is the key reference in terms of revenue. Investors will analyze whether the supplier is gaining or losing market share. Trends in volume and price are also important. Many suppliers provide this information on a geographical basis, as do the car manufacturers. **Exhibit 72**, component supplier Valeo's full year 2014 sales performance, highlights clear outperformance in all its main operating regions except South America.

In terms of margin performance, as with car manufacturers, investors tend to look mainly at EBIT margin. Often, a breakdown occurs in the usual correlation between EBIT margins and ROIC. In component supply, a low EBIT margin can occur simultaneously with a high ROIC. An assembly business is low value added but also low in capital intensity, which means that high returns on capital employed can often be earned as long as asset turnover is high. This case is often true in assembly businesses. Arguably, ROIC is more important as a benchmark than EBIT margin because ROIC designates the amount of value creation in the business whereas EBIT margin is a return on sales. Investors should not assume that a business is either poor quality or not worthy of investing in on the basis of a low EBIT margin.

Exhibit 72. Valeo's Organic Sales Growth, 2014 Year-on-Year

Country	OEM Sales Growth[a]	Outperformance[b]
China	–18.0%	–12.0%
Europe	8	8
Asia (ex China)	–3	1
North America	7	3
South America	–15	–4
World	7.0	6.2

[a]Valeo's organic growth rate.
[b]Versus car production in each region.
Source: Jacques Aschenbroich, "2014 Results," Valeo presentation (24 February 2015): www.valeo.com/medias/upload/2015/02/78396/2014-results-presentation.pdf.

Another investor misconception relates to generation of free cash flow (FCF, defined as operating cash flow adjusted for working capital movements, minus capital expenditures). Investors sometimes place undue emphasis on FCF generation, almost as if it were the same as value creation. Such emphasis is not the best approach because it takes a short-term view of the company and its industry. It also does not capture the long-term benefits of the investment cycle. For example, in the tire manufacturing business, capacity is being expanded quite aggressively in emerging markets, capital intensity might be expected to be high, and the ability to spin off FCF is low. FCF generation depends on the part of the investment cycle that a tire company happens to find itself in.

VALUATION METRICS

CAR MANUFACTURERS

Given the volatility of earnings and difficulty in forecasting them, investors have tended to avoid valuation metrics involving multiples of earnings, apart from P/E, which is a universally popular metric for valuing shares.

Most car manufacturers have their own leasing and finance divisions, which are usually split out by the companies in their disclosures. Therefore, investors sometimes value the two parts separately. Typically, an earnings multiple can be applied to the manufacturing (or "industrial") part of the business. The rule of thumb for valuing the leasing or finance division is 1.0× book value. Currently, leasing and finance operations are highly profitable because of low loan default rates and low loan loss provisions relative to historical averages. In theory, therefore, a significant premium to book value could be justified, although investors rarely attribute a valuation of more than 1.2× book value to the leasing and finance division. Alternatively, investors can also choose to value the entire company as one unit, which facilitates the calculations and simplifies the approach.

For a car manufacturer, P/E has its limitations as a measure of value. It is used mostly for comparing companies within the automotive industry at a particular time, as opposed to comparing a company through time. Also, P/E is influenced by the part of the business cycle we find ourselves in: If earnings are thought to be close to peak, investors can expect P/Es to be low, and vice versa, as the market discounts the expected future trend in earnings. This characteristic is typical of any cyclical company.

Furthermore, car manufacturers' balance sheets can be of varying quality. Some, particularly the premium German and Japanese manufacturers, harbor large amounts of net cash, while others carry large amounts of net debt. In an environment of low interest rates, these differences are not appropriately accounted for by the use of P/E. Using P/E is a simplistic approach to valuation. Typical P/E multiples in the automotive industry, especially for the mass-market manufacturers, are single digits, but they can reach low double digits depending on market perceptions of share quality and associated risk factors.

The cyclicality of the business also renders discounted cash flow (DCF) analysis difficult, and this technique does not lend itself well to the manufacturing sector. Similarly, earnings multiples—EBIT or EBITDA—are rarely used because of high earnings cyclicality, although they sometimes feature in valuation tables.

Valuation by multiples of sales makes more sense than valuation by earnings multiples because sales are less volatile than earnings. A popular measure is enterprise value to sales (EV/sales), which also takes into account different quality balance sheets in the sector. One must be careful to correctly calculate EV by adjusting for the market value of minorities and associates and taking into account off-balance-sheet items, such as pension deficits. In particular, what needs to be accounted for is the amount of industrial net debt—that is, the net debt of the car business alone, aside from any finance or leasing division.

EV/sales for the automotive manufacturing industry has averaged about 0.3× in recent years, but a great deal of variability accompanies this average. Some stocks exhibit negative EV for several consecutive years, while others' EV is comfortably higher, reaching 0.4× or even 0.5×. A prime example of a negative-EV stock was Renault for a number of years, because its stake in Nissan was not properly valued by the market and it suffered a chronic discount for being perceived as having a holding company structure.

In these circumstances, an investor might use a sum-of-the-parts approach—that is, valuing a car company on the basis of its car manufacturing operations and adding in the value of any stakes held in other companies. The challenge is to determine whether any hidden value uncovered by this approach will be valued by the market. Discounts of share prices to their intrinsic values can persist for years because of, among other factors, market perceptions of risk and earnings quality.

Multiples of book value tend not to be widely used, apart from Japanese automotive manufacturers. This phenomenon is cultural. Price to book value (P/BV) has the advantage that book value does not vary as much as earnings, so it is applicable to such cyclical industries as automotive manufacturing. Most automotive manufacturers are trading on P/BV multiples of at least 1.0×, rarely exceeding 1.5×. For Japanese manufacturers, a discount to book value tends to highlight undervaluation in some instances, and usually, the stocks return to 1.0× book value or higher.

Dividend yield can provide an indication of when a car stock is approaching a floor or ceiling valuation. If earnings estimates are still credible and the expected dividend is still likely to be paid, then the dividend yield will become more attractive. The reverse is also true: A rising share price not accompanied by an increase in earnings estimates or increase in the dividend expectation leads to a lower dividend yield, making the stock less attractive to buy or own. Dividend yield as a measure tends to be favored by income funds and is most useful in stable economic times, when an inflection point in the economic cycle that will significantly change or jeopardize payment of the dividend is unlikely. A dividend yield of 3% or more would be considered attractive.

As noted previously, car industry investors pay considerable attention to free cash flow but FCF generation should not be confused with value creation. Generation of FCF is almost a requirement from the viewpoint of long-term business sustainability, but for a small number of years, ambitious expansion plans may deprive a company of its ability to generate positive FCF. Short-term-minded investors can be quite impatient with a company that is not generating positive FCF, which may be an impediment to such investors buying the stock. For this reason, announcement of a future period's capex budget is often eagerly awaited by parts of the investment community.

COMPONENT SUPPLIERS AND TIRE MANUFACTURERS

The segment of component suppliers and tire manufacturers has some key differences from automotive manufacturing with regard to valuation. The supplier side of the automotive market has the advantage of simpler accounting and corporate structures: They have no finance or leasing businesses distorting the consolidated accounts and usually have fewer stakes in other companies (outside of the *chaebol* and *keiretsu* structures).

P/E tends to be a universally popular valuation metric for investors in these businesses, even though earnings of automotive suppliers are highly cyclical. Tire manufacturers have the least cyclical earnings in the entire automotive chain because most of their earnings come from replacement tires, whose demand pattern is less volatile through the economic cycle.

As in the case of car manufacturers, P/Es in these businesses tend to be in single digits, although they can reach low double digits or even mid-teens in the case of fast-growth suppliers with a technological edge. This scenario of P/Es includes tire manufacturers, which tend to trade at a premium to other car suppliers because of the lower cyclicality of their earnings, good pricing power, and healthy margins and returns on capital.

Valuation multiples based on sales, such as EV/sales, are rarely used in these segments. The reason is the varying differences in margins within the supplier sector, from barely profitable or loss-making companies to highly profitable ones. Thus, an EV/sales comparison is useless because it is influenced by profitability. EV/EBITDA and EV/EBIT are sometimes used, however, even if profit aggregates are subject to the risk of significant and unexpected revision as a result of high earnings cyclicality.

DCF analysis tends to be more favored for valuing suppliers than automotive manufacturers, even though automotive suppliers, aside from tire manufacturers, are not any less cyclical than car manufacturers.

Multiples, such as P/BV, are rarely used outside Japan, which has adopted this measure as a regular valuation metric.

Dividend yield is sometimes an indicator of whether a stock is close to its floor or ceiling valuation, so it can be a buying or selling signal. This indicator is most popular with income funds. The ability to pay a dividend usually signals that cash generation is adequate, which appeals to investors with concerns for positive FCF generation.

For more information on global auto assemblers' valuations and global auto suppliers' and tire makers' valuations, please see **Exhibit A.1** and **Exhibit A.2**, respectively, in the Appendix.

INDUSTRY RESOURCES

INDUSTRY ORGANIZATIONS

1. Society of Motor Manufacturers and Traders: www.smmt.co.uk
2. International Organization of Motor Vehicle Manufacturers: www.oica.net
3. International Council on Clean Transportation: www.theicct.org
4. European Automobile Manufacturers Association: www.acea.be
5. Association of Car Rental Industry Systems Standards: www.acriss.org
6. US Council for Automotive Research LLC: www.uscar.org
7. Original Equipment Suppliers Association: www.oesa.org
8. Motor & Equipment Manufacturers Association: www.mema.org
9. Alliance of Auto Manufacturers: www.autoalliance.org
10. International Federation of Automotive Engineering Societies: www.fisita.com
11. China Association of Automobile Manufacturers: www.caam.org.cn/english
12. Center for Automotive Research: www.cargroup.org
13. Society of Automotive Analysts: www.saaautoleaders.org
14. Insurance Institute for Highway Safety: www.iihs.org
15. Verband der Automobilindustrie: www.vda.de/en
16. Automotive Aftermarket Suppliers Association: www.aftermarketsuppliers.org
17. Electric Drive Transportation Association: www.electricdrive.org
18. Asociación Española de Fabricantes de Autómoviles y Camiones: www.anfac.com
19. Rubber & Plastics News: www.rubbernews.com

GOVERNMENT ORGANIZATIONS

1. US Department of Transportation: www.dot.gov
2. US Bureau of Transportation Statistics: www.rita.dot.gov/bts
3. US Department of Commerce, Bureau of Economic Analysis: www.bea.gov
4. US Census Bureau (data on automotive industry): www.census.gov
5. US National Highway Traffic Safety Administration: www.nhtsa.gov
6. US Environmental Protection Agency: www.epa.gov
7. US Bureau of Labor Statistics: www.bls.gov
8. US Federal Reserve Economic Research and Data: www.federalreserve.gov/econresdata
9. US Department of Energy, Energy Efficiency & Renewable Energy: www.fueleconomy.gov
10. National Bureau of Statistics of China: www.stats.gov.cn/english
11. Brazilian Institute of Geography and Statistics: www.ibge.gov.br/english
12. European Commission Automotive Industry: http://ec.europa.eu/enterprise/sectors/automotive/index_en.htm

AUTOMOBILE INDUSTRY CONSULTANTS

1. The Economist Intelligence Unit: www.eiu.com
2. IHS Automotive Industry Solutions: www.ihs.com/industry/automotive/index.aspx
3. WardsAuto: www.wardsauto.com
4. LMC Automotive: www.lmc-auto.com
5. J.D. Power (for model ratings and surveys): www.jdpower.com
6. McKinsey & Company: www.mckinsey.com
7. Frost & Sullivan: ww2.frost.com/research/industry/automotive-transportation

OTHER RESOURCES

1. SlideShare (search for presentations on the automotive sector): www.slideshare.net
2. Auto Trends Magazine: www.autotrends.org
3. Inside EVs: http://insideevs.com
4. Website on plug-in electric cars: www.plugincars.com/guides.html

APPENDIX

Exhibit A.1. Global Auto Assemblers' Valuations

Company Name (market cap, billions)	Current Price	P/E			EV/EBITDA			FCF Yield (%)			EV/Sales			EBIT Margin (%)		
		2015E	2016E	2017E	2015E	2016E	2017E	2015E	2016E	2017E	2015E	2016E	2017E	2015E	2016E	2017E
European automakers																
BMW AG (€64.45)	EUR 98.18	10.37	9.74	9.42	3.61	3.34	3.13	5.54	5.15	4.89	0.60	0.56	0.53	10.82	10.89	10.76
Daimler AG (€87.34)	EUR 81.64	10.93	9.75	9.10	4.17	3.64	3.24	5.97	5.12	4.58	0.51	0.47	0.43	8.54	9.16	9.41
Fiat Chrysler Automobiles N.V. (€16.91)	EUR 13.14	15.70	9.96	7.25	3.15	2.82	2.38	6.90	6.00	4.85	0.28	0.27	0.24	4.00	4.46	4.91
Peugeot SA (€14.21)	EUR 18.45	17.03	11.48	8.90	3.23	2.52	1.93	7.64	5.39	3.78	0.25	0.21	0.17	3.22	3.83	4.38
Porsche Automobil Holding SE Pref (€23.14)	EUR 75.57	6.73	5.92	5.22	N/A	N/A	N/A	N/A	N/A	29.81	N/A	N/A	N/A	N/A	N/A	N/A
Renault SA (€27.39)	EUR 93.42	10.19	8.19	7.17	5.30	4.66	4.28	11.90	9.46	8.61	0.58	0.53	0.49	4.89	5.60	5.65
Volkswagen AG (€98.95)	EUR 207.55	8.67	7.77	7.15	2.85	2.47	2.10	5.86	4.90	4.06	0.38	0.35	0.31	6.46	7.04	7.58
US automakers																
Ford Motor Company (€53.81)	USD 15.01	9.42	7.96	7.44	4.72	3.84	3.74	8.80	6.62	6.08	0.37	0.34	0.32	4.21	5.09	5.23
General Motors Company (€47.95)	USD 33.33	7.43	6.48	5.80	2.74	2.47	2.23	4.15	3.69	3.97	0.27	0.26	0.24	6.49	6.91	5.98
Chinese automakers																
BYD Co. Ltd. Class H (€13.43)	HKD 46.55	43.28	34.76	28.55	16.04	13.91	12.23	33.07	25.65	22.18	1.99	1.69	1.52	6.02	6.59	6.83
Brilliance China Auto (€7.09)	HKD 12.10	8.85	7.36	5.96	N/A	N/A	N/A	N/A	N/A	N/A	7.17	6.73	5.89	(4.69)	(4.25)	14.01
Dongfeng Automobile Co. Ltd. Class A (€13.04)	CNY 12.68	25.83	16.55	13.91	N/A	N/A	N/A	N/A	N/A	N/A	N/A	N/A	N/A	2.20	3.54	3.80
Geely Automobile Holdings Limited (€4.25)	HKD 4.14	11.30	9.00	7.59	5.61	4.43	3.49	7.57	5.92	4.52	0.82	0.64	0.48	10.82	10.82	10.72
Great Wall Motor Co., Ltd. Class H (€13.47)	HKD 38.00	7.87	6.41	5.73	7.15	5.63	4.68	8.18	6.36	5.34	1.31	1.04	0.88	16.01	16.32	16.39
Guangzhou Auto Group, Class H (€5.38)	HKD 7.18	9.59	7.98	6.77	91.75	66.88	52.44	N/A	N/A	N/A	3.08	2.68	2.39	(0.93)	(0.31)	0.10

(continued)

Exhibit A.1. Global Auto Assemblers' Valuations (continued)

Company Name (market cap, billions)	Current Price	P/E			EV/EBITDA			FCF Yield (%)			EV/Sales			EBIT Margin (%)		
		2015E	2016E	2017E	2015E	2016E	2017E	2015E	2016E	2017E	2015E	2016E	2017E	2015E	2016E	2017E
Japanese automakers																
Daihatsu Motor Co., Ltd. (€5.44)	JPY 1,743	12.06	10.98	10.60	3.42	3.03	2.85	5.94	5.17	4.76	0.34	0.32	0.30	5.71	6.11	6.24
Fuji Heavy Industries Ltd. (€25.77)	JPY 4,508	9.95	9.55	9.08	4.76	4.31	4.14	5.47	4.99	4.81	0.95	0.84	0.79	17.31	16.91	16.51
Honda Motor Co., Ltd. (€52.31)	JPY 3,962	11.56	9.96	8.90	9.33	8.34	6.09	15.07	12.59	9.05	0.85	0.79	0.61	5.63	6.29	6.69
Mazda Motor Corp. (€10.51)	JPY 2,398	9.03	7.99	7.53	4.92	4.11	3.53	6.73	5.56	4.76	0.47	0.41	0.36	6.94	7.37	7.59
Mitsubishi Motors Corporation (€7.51)	JPY 1,042	8.96	8.80	8.29	3.33	2.79	2.31	4.79	3.99	3.30	0.29	0.26	0.23	6.13	6.53	6.89
Nissan Motor Co., Ltd. (€39.17)	JPY 1,275	10.26	9.12	8.22	9.27	8.61	6.84	16.39	15.00	11.70	0.96	0.94	0.79	5.88	6.28	6.76
Suzuki Motor Corp. (€16.99)	JPY 4,135	18.72	16.39	15.35	4.17	3.47	3.51	7.32	5.92	5.84	0.48	0.41	0.42	6.51	6.86	7.23
Toyota Motor Corp. (€189.05)	JPY 8,203	10.48	9.62	8.88	10.15	7.90	6.91	13.60	10.54	9.15	1.51	1.21	1.07	11.10	11.45	11.71
Other Asian automakers																
Hyundai Motor Company (€31.34)	KRW 136,000	4.92	4.68	4.41	5.76	5.36	4.86	8.13	7.61	6.91	0.64	0.61	0.56	7.81	8.03	8.09
KIA Motors Corporation (€14.70)	KRW 45,300	5.99	5.53	5.12	4.07	3.44	3.25	6.55	5.48	5.03	0.33	0.30	0.28	5.07	5.41	5.57
Mahindra and Mahindra Ltd. (€10.82)	INR 1,281	21.96	17.72	15.75	15.35	12.23	10.74	18.83	14.75	13.31	1.81	1.52	1.30	9.62	10.29	9.80
Maruti Suzuki India Limited (€17.31)	INR 4,023	22.87	17.75	15.02	12.84	9.97	8.38	17.96	13.24	11.08	1.94	1.55	1.32	10.77	11.73	11.90
Tata Motors Limited (€20.52)	INR 434.6	7.65	6.23	5.61	3.35	2.82	2.62	5.39	4.54	4.36	0.55	0.46	0.43	10.13	10.09	9.84

Note: E = estimate; N/A = not available.

Sources: Citi; data are based on consensus estimates as at 1 July 2015. Market cap data are sourced from Morningstar (www.morningstar.co.uk) and translated into euros using www.xe.com.

Exhibit A.2. Global Auto Suppliers' and Tire Makers' Valuations

Company Name (market cap, billions)	Currrent Price	PE			EV/EBITDA			FCF Yield (%)			EV/Sales			EBIT Margin (%)		
		2015E	2016E	2017E	2015E	2016E	2017E	2015E	2016E	2017E	2015E	2016E	2017E	2015E	2016E	2017E
European suppliers																
Autoliv Inc. (€9.28)	USD 116.75	18.35	15.66	14.02	8.97	8.15	7.52	12.13	10.93	9.99	1.17	1.09	1.03	9.61	10.01	10.31
Continental AG (€42.45)	EUR 212.25	15.22	13.84	12.87	7.61	6.79	6.23	10.69	9.45	8.62	1.19	1.08	0.99	11.14	11.48	11.50
Faurecia SA (€4.57)	EUR 36.89	13.17	10.46	9.27	4.13	3.46	3.10	7.01	5.69	5.04	0.29	0.26	0.23	4.10	4.51	4.61
GKN plc (€7.90)	GBP 3.35	12.70	11.52	10.87	6.83	6.17	5.58	9.38	8.33	7.50	0.79	0.74	0.69	8.45	8.82	9.22
Valeo SA (€10.99)	EUR 141.35	15.51	13.43	11.90	6.74	5.91	5.23	10.92	9.35	8.10	0.81	0.73	0.65	7.39	7.76	7.97
US suppliers																
BorgWarner Inc. (€11.73)	USD 56.84	17.59	14.63	12.46	9.70	8.38	7.14	12.44	10.55	9.01	1.65	1.45	1.28	13.23	13.74	14.16
Johnson Controls, Inc. (€29.70)	USD 49.53	14.54	12.50	10.96	10.43	9.44	7.90	13.61	12.27	10.31	1.01	1.02	0.95	7.45	8.32	9.19
Lear Corporation (€7.88)	USD 112.26	11.66	10.18	9.18	6.07	5.45	4.72	7.91	7.03	6.08	0.52	0.47	0.43	6.54	6.74	7.06
Magna International Inc. (€20.67)	CAD 70.10	12.25	10.14	8.91	7.14	6.61	6.11	9.82	8.97	8.17	0.73	0.70	0.65	7.43	7.83	7.96
Japanese suppliers																
Aisin Seiki Co. Ltd. (€10.78)	JPY 5,210	14.37	12.90	11.62	4.00	3.60	3.18	7.80	6.89	6.03	0.48	0.45	0.41	6.19	6.55	6.87
Calsonic Kansei Corporation (€1.71)	JPY 871	9.99	9.27	8.52	3.64	3.17	2.84	6.09	5.14	4.48	0.22	0.19	0.18	3.58	3.79	3.94
Denso Corp. (€35.61)	JPY 6,096	16.03	14.56	13.50	7.31	6.62	5.88	11.74	10.37	9.18	1.04	0.97	0.89	8.89	9.35	9.67
Keihin Corp. (€0.95)	JPY 1,756	9.65	8.67	8.34	2.33	1.95	1.62	4.06	3.24	2.66	0.29	0.24	0.20	7.08	7.43	7.49
Koito Manufacturing Co., Ltd. (€5.62)	JPY 4,775	18.15	16.11	14.58	6.78	5.90	5.01	9.65	8.34	7.06	0.88	0.79	0.69	9.10	9.45	9.74
Nissin Kogyo Co., Ltd. (€0.96)	JPY 2,021	11.30	10.32	9.26	2.88	2.39	1.90	4.39	3.63	2.85	0.37	0.32	0.26	8.39	8.73	9.24
NOK Corporation (€4.81)	JPY 3,800	14.01	13.31	12.47	5.80	5.28	4.79	9.37	8.49	7.51	0.81	0.74	0.66	8.65	8.72	8.82

(continued)

Exhibit A.2. Global Auto Suppliers' and Tire Makers' Valuations (continued)

Company Name (market cap, billions)	Currrent Price	PE			EV/EBITDA			FCF Yield (%)			EV/Sales			EBIT Margin (%)		
		2015E	2016E	2017E	2015E	2016E	2017E	2015E	2016E	2017E	2015E	2016E	2017E	2015E	2016E	2017E
Japanese suppliers (continued)																
Stanley Electric Co., Ltd. (€3.13)	JPY 2,552	13.71	12.13	11.41	5.38	4.78	4.26	8.54	7.49	6.60	1.01	0.93	0.84	11.87	12.36	12.80
Toyota Industries Corp. (€16.06)	JPY 6,980	16.22	14.77	13.83	10.89	9.72	8.81	19.57	17.12	15.31	1.19	1.09	1.02	6.06	6.39	6.66
Other Asian suppliers																
Bharat Forge Ltd. (€3.67)	INR 1,063	26.10	20.06	17.52	14.38	11.29	9.83	17.96	13.71	12.31	2.96	2.43	2.17	16.50	17.72	17.60
Hyundai Mobis Co., Ltd. (€16.01)	KRW 212,000	5.93	5.50	5.19	4.52	3.89	3.33	5.35	4.61	3.93	0.43	0.38	0.33	8.13	8.29	8.33
Tire makers																
Bridgestone Corporation (€25.97)	JPY 4,528	10.32	9.74	9.36	4.92	4.59	4.31	6.80	6.32	5.93	0.93	0.87	0.81	13.63	13.70	13.67
Goodyear Tire & Rubber Company (€7.43)	USD 30.15	10.11	8.49	7.94	4.88	4.42	3.99	6.72	6.03	5.59	0.73	0.69	0.61	10.78	11.46	10.98
Hankook Tire Co., Ltd. (€4.31)	KRW 42,000	8.47	7.73	7.19	5.22	4.74	4.25	8.28	7.49	6.67	1.14	1.02	0.90	13.73	13.63	13.46
Michelin SCA (€17.46)	EUR 93.99	11.76	10.69	9.91	4.81	4.50	4.13	7.06	6.56	6.04	0.87	0.83	0.78	12.37	12.70	12.85
Nokian Renkaat Oyj (€3.74)	EUR 28.11	18.28	15.54	13.60	9.48	8.69	7.84	12.27	11.00	9.75	2.63	2.45	2.25	21.46	22.31	23.08
Pirelli & C. S.p.A. (€7.36)	EUR 15.14	15.99	13.41	12.10	6.63	5.93	5.31	8.85	7.88	7.00	1.30	1.19	1.08	14.72	15.07	15.35
Sumitomo Rubber Industries, Ltd. (€3.66)	JPY 1,897	8.87	8.64	8.00	5.23	4.85	4.48	7.96	7.39	6.72	0.81	0.76	0.71	10.14	10.28	10.54
Yokohama Rubber Co. Ltd. (€2.86)	JPY 2,458	9.52	8.80	8.27	5.84	5.38	4.99	8.53	8.03	7.50	0.84	0.80	0.75	9.83	9.93	10.05

Note: E = estimate.
Sources: Citi; data are based on consensus estimates as at 1 July 2015. Market cap data are sourced from Morningstar (www.morningstar.co.uk) and translated into euros using www.xe.com.

Made in the USA
Las Vegas, NV
07 November 2026

57673718R00057